Always Within

Grieving the Loss of Your Infant

Melissa Eshleman

Original Edition

Find Your Way Publishing, Inc.
PO Box 667
Norway, Maine

Always Within

Grieving The Loss of Your Infant

First Edition

Published by Find Your Way Publishing, Inc.

PO BOX 667

Norway, ME 04268 U.S.A.

www.findyourwaypublishing.com

The stories contained in this book have been edited, yet not so to distort or lose any intended emotion or meaning submitted by its contributor, used by permission. A portion of this book was taken from the book *The Gift Nobody Wants* by Janine A Milliken, used by permission.

Cover, interior design and layout by Kimberly Martin

Scripture quotations are taken from the King James Version of the Bible. Public domain.

ISBN-13: 978-0-9824692-4-8

ISBN-10: 0-9824692-4-1

Library of Congress Control Number: 2010927345

Printed in the United States of America

To my husband, Ed:
I love sharing my life with you.
To our children,
Paige, Wyatt, Marrae, & William:
You are all amazing
and bring me immense joy!
I love you so much.
To our son, Lucas,
who blessed us with his presence for four days.
To my parents, family, & friends:
You have taught me so much;
I am forever grateful.

And to all the parents who have
experienced the loss of a child:
You are not alone
and your tears will not go unseen.

With Gratitude

Deepest thanks to the parents who had the courage to share their heartfelt experiences and stories. I am so touched and honored to work with you. By your example and with your words, you have shown the rest of us that we are not alone. And that with faith, perseverance, and hope, healing - although a work in progress - is a realistic goal to attain. It is my hope that you found some solace and healing as you bravely wrote about your loss. I believe our angels are with us, guiding us to be true to ourselves and helping us see the beauty in all things, including loss. I am truly grateful and wish you all the best.

Special thanks to Jackie Rybeck for being so wonderful. Without your expertise, enthusiasm and humor, I would not have been able to finish this project.

I appreciate all the experiences that life has brought my way and the knowledge and wisdom that I have gained through all of them. I appreciate every single person who is and has been a part of my life, as you have contributed to the growth of my spirit and soul.

Deep, humble appreciation goes to the Divine Source; my Great Creator, in whom I grow closer to every day. There are no words to describe the joy, wonder and awe I continue to feel as I study the Word of God. Thank you for always hearing my prayers, for easing my pain and heartaches, for washing away my worries, for teaching me to trust the Universe always, for sincere and endless forgiveness and for endless blessings. I am moved and blessed by the daily miracles in my life.

Foreword

The obituary stated four days. I never really understood that. May 17, 2001 – May 20, 2001. Isn't that three days? It was counted as four individual days; the 17th, 18th, 19th, and 20th. I was happy for the fourth day, but his life was significant regardless. He was loved by so many people. Does that sound strange? That Lucas was loved by so many people even though he only lived for four days? It's amazing isn't it? There is no explanation for love; it just is. Lucas touched so many lives in the short time that he was here on this earth. A short stay, yet a huge impact; he made an enormous difference.

Lucas died in our arms a few days after he was born. It was not suppose to happen that way. The emotions that raged through me during that time were overwhelming, an all-encompassing void that I didn't know what to do with. I've never felt so alone. I felt as though no one could possibly understand how empty I felt. Everyone seemed to be going about their business and I was lost in grief. I had no idea what to do or who to turn to. I finally found an online infant-loss group. I signed up to receive emails and for a year I just read posts from other grieving parents. Until one day, with a little apprehension, I finally shared my story. The group helped me with my grief; reading and responding to my emails, sharing their stories and by reaching out with encouraging words of compassion and understanding. The group helped me realize that, at a time when I felt more alone than ever, I wasn't alone in my pain and heartache. A sense of comfort came over me that I hadn't experienced before. I realized that my experience and words were helping others. It was in that moment that I became aware that I wanted to, no I needed to do something to help others who have or will have to endure the grief and confusion that comes with losing an infant. So I decided to write a book; a book that would include stories from people who have experienced the loss of a child, because for me that is what seemed to help the most. This is a clear and easy-to-understand book to help people and their families realize that they are not alone in their grief; a book of hope.

Losing Lucas has taken me on a journey that I wasn't expecting. I miss him, and what would have been, every day. Since his death, I can't help but look at things differently. Things that matter the most have become clearer; a bit of the fog has lifted. I have come to realize that the little things in life bring me the most joy....watching my children sleep, hearing my children laugh, my slippers, my first cup of coffee in the morning, a warm breeze on my face, the sound of the rain, being in nature, a hot bath...these simple things satisfy my soul. I'm appreciative of the simplest moments. I am continually learning to trust God and to have faith in all of it.

It is my hope that this book and the heartfelt stories shared by parents who have been there, will bring comfort to those who have suffered the loss of a pregnancy, an infant, a sibling, a grandchild; a loved one.

These pages offer sincere advice, encouragement and inspiration. May this book be a gentle reminder that although you may feel it, you are not alone; may you be blessed with peace and comfort.

"Imagine a love so strong
that saying hello and goodbye
in the same day
was worth the sorrow."

Author Unknown

Contents

About This Book

This is not just a book of hope. It is a book about an incredible love that cannot be broken or severed. It is an easy-to-understand book that doesn't tell you how you should feel; rather it explains the many different experiences and feelings that can follow a miscarriage or infant loss. If you want to read all the way through from cover to cover you can, but it's also broken down in a way that can be used as a helpful and comforting reference or guide. Through other's stories, it offers guidance on how to deal with your emotions, how to keep your infants memory alive, along with other helpful and inspiring thoughts and ideas.

Coping with miscarriage or infant loss can be one of the most difficult trials in a person's life and one most of us are unprepared to face. Pregnancy and infant loss are the most unexpected losses; they don't fit into the natural order of life.

With miscarriage or infant loss, hopes and dreams are shattered before they can even begin. We've been taught to never give up on our dreams; to dream big and keep dreaming, that all of our hopes and dreams can be obtained if we don't quit. But what do you do when your dream has ended before it had the chance to come into being or to begin? The dream is over and even though you've always been taught to never lose sight of your dreams, there appears to be absolutely no hope. How do you obtain a dream that has literally died? What can be done? What's the next step when faced with such a loss?

This book is like having a caring and compassionate support group in the palm of your hands. You will be moved by the deep, emotional honesty of these stories. This book offers practical advice and suggestions. Some stories will touch you more than others. Trust your feelings and take what comes to you on your own time. Wherever you are, on this challenging yet miraculous journey, you'll find that although it feels like it, you are not alone in your grief. And you will gain a little more strength with each passing day.

If you have suffered the devastating loss of a miscarriage or infant loss, or if you love someone who has experienced such a loss, you will want to read each of these heartfelt stories. This book is about the dark, stormy clouds slowly breaking. The sun is peaking through and it will shine again. Together let's move forward toward healing.

Always Within

Grieving the Loss of Your Infant

1

Ivy Rose Harris

Stillborn at 39 weeks on March 29, 2002

My Story:

My husband and I had a two-year-old daughter and we were thrilled to be expecting another little girl. My pregnancy was exceptionally healthy, normal and uneventful. One week before my due date, I woke up with contractions every 15 minutes. I anxiously called my midwife and was excited to make an appointment to be seen that afternoon; sure that she'd tell me this was it, that I'd soon be meeting my new baby girl!

When it came time for my appointment, I was examined by the midwife, who confirmed that I was in early labor, but something was wrong. She spent several minutes searching for the baby's heartbeat and called in another midwife and then the physician to check too. I was terrified. They rushed me into the ultrasound facility where the technician confirmed that my daughter had passed away. I was numb. There were so many decisions and arrangements and horrible phone calls to make and the next few hours were like a blur.

Labor progressed and I arrived at the hospital with my husband that evening. Several hours of contractions later, it was time to deliver my daughter. Pushing was difficult. Not physically, but because I knew that once she was born, I'd have to let her go. As long as I kept her inside, I still had her. I could still keep her. She was still mine.

But finally, reluctantly, through tears, Ivy Rose was born at 3 am on March 29, 2002. I kept my eyes closed through the delivery and when the midwife urged me to take her in my arms after the birth, I was so afraid to look. But I did. She was beautiful! So perfect and so lovely, that it was easy for a few moments to forget why we were so sad. I fell in love with her instantly. It was not at all different than I felt after the birth of my first daughter, or my subsequent children. I loved her dearly and I was overjoyed to meet her.

We admired her and held her for several hours until I knew it was time to let her go. That was so hard. I knew I'd never see her again and I thought to myself: *Why can't I just keep her? Why can't I take her home? She's mine.*

The next few days were the worst of my life. We had a small memorial service and a burial. My breasts were painfully full and I remember thinking that I wanted nothing more in the entire world just then, than to nurse a baby. I felt empty and exhausted and confused and angry.

I can't remember when it became easier. Hours turned to days without tears; then weeks. I forced myself to focus on the idea of conceiving again. I felt that the only way I could possibly go on; the only way to make something good come from Ivy's loss was to have another baby. We consulted doctors and specialists, who couldn't determine an exact cause of death, and chalked the stillbirth up to an umbilical cord accident.

The road to conceiving again was long and bumpy, but we did have another healthy, live baby in our arms two years later. And then two more babies after that. The weeks without tears have turned to months, but there isn't one single day that goes by that I don't remember Ivy, and think of how different my life would be if she were here.

The hardest thing for me was/is:

Dealing with the anger and bitterness at how unfair this was.

Helpful things that family and friends did that I will forever be grateful for:

Listening to me; just listening. Not offering platitudes or advice, just listening to me rant and rave and cry.

Things that have helped me cope and deal with the heartache:

It has been very helpful to meet other women online that have gone through similar experiences. Obviously, going on to have subsequent healthy pregnancies and babies has certainly been something that has brought me immense joy. I think very often that these are children who wouldn't be here otherwise.

What I have learned from this:

I have certainly learned not to take pregnancy or babies for granted and to cherish each moment with my children.

How I keep my infant's memory alive:

I don't have many tangible mementos of Ivy. I have her tiny hat she wore at the hospital and a certificate with her footprints. I look at these once or twice each year. I have a necklace that holds the birthstone of all my children, including Ivy's. This is very special to me.

Additional words to help others dealing with the loss of their infant:

Seek out others who have gone through something similar. Know that you are not alone and that you *will* get through this, as much as it seems like you won't or that you don't even want to. You can go on again; and experience happiness and joy again, but you'll always have that bit of sadness, no matter what.

~ Rachel Harris ~

He healeth the broken in heart,
and bindeth up their wounds.
He telleth the number of the stars;
he calleth them all by their names.
Great is our Lord, and of great power:
his understanding is infinite.
Psalms 147:3-5

2

Jessica Nicole Baity

April 8, 2007 (Easter day)

My Story:

In 2000 on New Year's Eve I had a miscarriage at about 37 weeks. It took almost a year and a half to get pregnant again with my son, who was born with a mild defect; a cleft lip in January 2003. He's had surgery and looks great and is healthy. I tried to get pregnant for about two-to-three years after my son turned approximately 18 months. After much prayer and other difficulties in life, I finally got pregnant with my daughter in late summer, 2006. The pregnancy was healthy. I had no issues at all during the pregnancy, except I had a lot of joint pain; so much that I could barely walk some days.

On Thursday, April 5th, I had my doctor's appointment and everything looked great, I was 37 weeks along. On Saturday, at the end of the day I realized I didn't feel any kicking that day, and my daughter was an extreme kicker, so I planned to monitor her kicks when I laid down for bed, but instead, I quickly fell asleep. I woke up Sunday, which was also Easter morning, to my husband making breakfast. After breakfast we hunted for Easter eggs with my 4-year-old son. I remember saying to him that next Easter he would be hunting eggs with his sister. I started dressing for church and remembered that I never monitored the kicks the previous night so I laid down to do so and didn't feel anything. I called the hospital and spoke to a nurse, she said to drink a sugary drink and lay down for 20-30 minutes and check for kicks and if I didn't feel anything to come in.

My husband took my son to church. If the testing turned out fine, I would join them when I was finished. If I needed to go in to the hospital, we could leave my son at church with his grandma, who would be there and take care of him. After 30-to-45 minutes I felt no kicks, so I called the hospital again and called my husband to come home. He arrived home and we went to the hospital. They hooked me up to the monitors and couldn't find a heartbeat. They started to look concerned. They paged the doctor, who wanted to do a sonogram to find out for sure. The doctor who wanted to do the sonogram lived 30 minutes away so we had to wait. She eventually arrived; she left her church service early to do the sonogram. My daughter was lying sideways and had no heartbeat. Seeing her sideways was weird since she had already started descending. But it made sense since I no longer felt the hard bump above my belly button where her butt usually was. My son had been born via C-section, and this one was a planned C-section, due April 23rd, so my doctor wanted to have a

C-section anyway. The doctor said we could do it that day or wait, but we wanted it over as soon as possible. I had eaten breakfast, so we had to wait a few hours before the surgery for digestion.

Those few hours were the worst. It really seemed like a nightmare. Friends from church had come and our family too, but coincidentally they all left the hospital at the same time and my husband went to eat lunch and get my son settled at Nana's house. I was alone in the hospital room and I really felt I was going to go crazy. I felt like screaming or running away, jumping out the window held some possibilities... but I was hooked up to monitors. I called my husband and he came back right away before eating. We spent the next couple hours crying and preparing. They decided to start early since I had eaten a very small breakfast. It was scary having surgery, knowing the horrible outcome. They took her out and weighed her and measured her, she was 7lbs., 11ozs. at 37 weeks. I imagine if she had made it to 40 weeks she would have been a nine-pounder like her brother. I didn't know what to expect when they brought her over, but the only words that came out of my mouth were 'she's perfect.'

The hardest thing for me was/is:

Besides not taking my baby home from the hospital, the hardest thing was coming home to a house full of baby stuff. We had the crib set up and baby clothes, blankets and so many things that we had purchased for our daughter. Luckily, we hadn't opened any of these things, so they could be taken to the store for a refund. We were so fortunate that friends did this task for us. The thought of going to the store and explaining why I was returning a large amount of baby goods was too much. Having friends and extended family to help in these mundane tasks is a life saver to you.

Helpful things that family and friends did that I will forever be grateful for:

Besides helping in the returning of the baby items, one thing that stands out in my memory is a friend, Wendy. She is so kind and giving. While I was in the hospital, she brought me a box of very soft tissues. All hospitals have tissues available, but they are very cheap and scratchy. I was just amazed at this little thing that she did, which meant so much to me. Friends and family essentially took over my life for the next couple weeks. Friends from church came and brought us dinner each night so we didn't have to think about that. Family came over and did our chores and laundry. It was scary knowing that someone else was doing things that were "our jobs," but in the end I was so grateful for the assistance. They also took care of my son, who was four at the time. He was with different people each day. Knowing that he was safe and with other children he could play with, allowed me to recuperate from the physical pain of the C-section, and allowed me to start to grieve without having to deal with a small child.

Things that have helped me cope and deal with the heartache:

Dealing with this kind of loss is different for everyone. What got me through each day was scrap-booking the good times of my son and family, prior to the loss. I didn't realize it at the time, but my husband noticed that I was remembering good times, to help pass the time during the bad times. The worst thing was having "free time" for my brain. If I didn't busy myself in some way, I would go straight to thinking about the loss and the questions and dwelling on bad thoughts and crying. It physically hurts to cry so much, so I tried to do things to avoid crying. I have also learned to pray more often. Prayer can be very soothing. Having someone to talk with is essential during your grieving process and the Heavenly Father understands all you are going through.

What I have learned from this:

That I am not alone. I have many friends and family members there for me, even though I didn't realize it before my loss. I am grateful for them, for the kindness and compassion I have received is a true blessing.

How I keep my infant's memory alive:

Since my daughter was stillborn, we do not have any "nice" pictures of her. We have one photo framed and while it is not on display, it is there when we need to see her. We think about her often. I have gotten to the point where I can just think about her and talk about her and not cry. It has been two-and-a-half years now. I kept everything about her, from the clothing she wore in the hospital, to all of the cards I received in sympathy, to other souvenirs. Periodically, I feel the need to look through them, knowing I will cry a lot, but I do it anyway. We don't visit the grave site very often, we don't feel the need to, but we do go visit her on her birthday and bring her flowers.

Additional words to help others dealing with the loss of their infant:

It's hard to believe it, but you will survive. At first I felt the despair and depression that comes with infant loss. You think you will feel this forever. Time does truly heal wounds. It won't be soon, not next week or next month or even in six months, but eventually you will move on. There will always be a hole in your heart for your baby, but there are other people in this life that need you, and you need to be the best you, you can be for them, especially if you have other children.

Your baby is being cared for by the Heavenly Father and Jesus. I know that since I am unable to care for her, who better to care for her then the Savior. We try to live our lives righteously, so that we can be with her again someday. I know I am needed here, to take care of my son, but knowing that one day I will be reunited with my angel, is a true comfort.

~ Fran Baity ~

I have not turned my back on you
So there is no need to cry.
I'm watching you from heaven
Just beyond the morning sky.
I've seen you almost fall apart
When you could barely stand.
I asked an angel to comfort you
And watched her take your hand.
She told me you are in more pain
Than I could ever be.
She wiped her eyes and swallowed hard
Then gave your hand to me.
Although you may not feel my touch
Or see me by your side.
I've whispered that I love you
While I wiped each tear you cried.
So please try not to ache for me
We'll meet again one day.
Beyond the dark and stormy sky
A rainbow lights thc way.

Author Unknown

3

Michael Joseph Skaggs

(We called him MJ)

July 25, 2009 - August 29, 2009

My Story:

After almost a year and a half and two rounds of the fertility medicine chlomid, my husband and I were absolutely elated when we found out we were expecting. My pregnancy started out just like any other, with the all-day morning sickness and nervousness of a first-time mother-to-be. We found out I was pregnant the beginning of December and by the beginning of January, I had started spotting. I was petrified that I was having a miscarriage and our doctor wanted us to come in and do an ultrasound to see what was going on.

We got the surprise of our life when we found out that not only were we having one baby, but there were two tiny babies growing in my belly! My husband, Willie, and I were in shock and could hardly speak we were so surprised. We spent the next few weeks overjoyed and eagerly anticipated the day we would find out what we were having. When I was 17 weeks pregnant, we had an ultrasound and both of our babies showed us 'the goods.' We were having two boys! And the doctor was pretty sure we were having identical twins! Two baby boys; we could just not be happier!

Four weeks later, we went in for another routine ultrasound. We got another shock that day, but not a good one. One of our babies looked to have a condition called CDH, or a congenital diaphragmatic hernia, but they weren't sure, so we would have to go to a specialist to confirm the diagnosis. Two weeks later we were devastated when we were told that, yes indeed Baby Boy B would have CDH. At this point we had decided to name our boys William Glen Skaggs IV and Michael Joseph Skaggs. We decided that our baby with CDH would be called Michael Joseph and we would call him MJ for short. At the time we had no clue what we would be in store for once our twins were born.

After numerous doctor appointments, specialists, ultrasounds, MRI's and everything else that needed to be done for a CDH baby in-utero, all we could do was wait. I developed preeclampsia at 34 weeks and was admitted into the hospital. I was put on bed rest with the goal of making it to 37 weeks; when I would be induced. Well, two weeks later, at 36 weeks my water broke and I was in labor! I was overjoyed to finally see my boys! After 26 hours of labor and two hours of pushing, I was nowhere near being able to push the boys out. So I had a C-section, and William Glen was born at 3:26 am and Michael Joseph was born at 3:27 am on July 25, 2009.

After my C-section I was unable to see MJ until 10 pm that evening. My son couldn't have looked more beautiful. However, he was very sick and we were very scared for him. After two days at the University of Kansas Medical Center, he was not showing any signs of improvement. Children's Mercy Hospital has a machine called ECMO, which is a heart and lung bypass. Since KU Med did not have this machine, and Children's did, MJ needed to be transferred to Children's. Watching him being moved was the scariest day of my life at that point.

The next day I was released from KU along with MJ's twin, Will. We rushed straight over to Children's and saw MJ. He looked much better at Children's and we got to bring Will in to see him every day, which was a life saver. It broke my heart thinking that my boys would be separated, but Children's made exceptions for twins and Will was allowed in to see MJ every day.

When MJ was six days old, he was placed on the ECMO machine. He was very ill and was unable to get off the ECMO machine and had his repair surgery on ECMO. After his surgery, MJ had a very rough few days. We thought we were going to lose him. But MJ pulled through and started to get better. When he was 31 days old, after 25 days on ECMO, MJ was strong enough to come off of the machine. Again, he had a rough few days, but on my birthday, August 28, he started to make a turn and really do well. At 4 pm that day, something happened and the doctors still don't know what.

We didn't leave the hospital that day and stayed by his side overnight. The next morning he was doing worse. Throughout the day the doctors did everything in their power to keep MJ alive. But then there was nothing else left to do. We made the choice to hold our son and let him know that we loved him in his final moments. The first time we held our son was the last. But we had three, amazing hours holding MJ and Will together. August 29, 2009 was the first time our family of four was together and we had to say good bye. MJ is gone, but he will never be forgotten. Thirty five days was not nearly enough, but he will remain in our hearts forever.

The hardest thing for me was/is:

We were, and still are, in a very unique situation of raising one baby and grieving the loss of another baby, all at the same time. I remember the first time I saw my surviving twin smile was two weeks after we lost his brother. I remember thinking, *Wow it's really taken this long for him to smile?* But all he knew was sadness, he probably had never seen me smile, his entire life at that point revolved around hospitals, surgeries, sadness, tears and death. We made a decision that night that we would have to put on a happy face for him. We would have to grieve on our own time; we would have to give our living son the best childhood that we could, no matter our pain. So we have put on a happy face for our living son. But the pain is still there, and it still hurts. Each moment is bittersweet; knowing what should be and what should have been.

One other baby-lost momma told me once, "You just gotta fake it till you make it." And that's what we do; we fake it till we make it.

Helpful things that family and friends did that I will forever be grateful for:

My sisters did so much for me in the first few days. I wanted so many things for his funeral service and they just did it, without thinking twice. That helped so much. The pictures that I have of MJ mean the world to me. We had Now I Lay Me Down To Sleep come and take professional pictures with us before and after MJ passed. My sisters went and framed a few of them and they looked so nice.

Things that have helped me cope and deal with the heartache:

We released 35 butterflies at MJ's service; one for each day that we had him with us on Earth. It is something that we plan on doing every August 29, the anniversary of his death. Now I see butterflies everywhere, and when I do, they remind me of him. We talk about him often, and have his pictures all over our house. I listen to a lot of music and hearing songs about loss have helped me, too. I can relate to the lyrics and it helps me release my pain. But the biggest thing that has helped me is blogging. I can say anything or feel anything and it's okay to put it out there. Getting every emotion out on paper helps me cope, especially with anger and sadness.

What I have learned from this:

I am a better mother because I lost my son. I hate to say that because sometimes it makes me feel like before I wasn't good enough to raise two babies. But it is the truth. I am more patient. I am calmer. I enjoy the little things. I have learned how to love deeper than I ever thought. My husband and I have become closer. But those things don't replace my son. They only make me love him more.

How I keep my infant's memory alive:

I have started a project in his name called MJ's Memories. MJ's Memories is part of a larger organization called Project Sweet Peas. Project Sweet Peas seeks to provide a little touch of comfort for parents of children in the intensive care units. This project was started by a group of parents who have one thing in common; we have all experienced what it is like having a critically ill child in the ICU. Through our experience we came together for support and comfort. Now it is our turn to give back. Our goal is simple: To provide gift bags that give a touch of comfort to someone in need and let them know they are not alone. We have been without MJ for six months now and we have donated 51 of these care packages to the hospital that MJ lived most of his life at. We are aiming to donate another 50 of these bags in two months. Providing other families with this comfort helps us heal and keep MJ's memory alive. My biggest fear in life is that MJ will be forgotten. By doing this I am ensuring that he won't.

Additional words to help others dealing with the loss of their infant:

Number one: It's not your fault. All the, could haves and should haves will never change the past. There's not a day that goes by that I don't think, *we could have done this, or we could have done that.* It's so hard not to, but please remember that it really is not your fault. Nothing you did or said or thought contributed to your baby's death. Instead, focus on the time you spent with your baby; in your belly and after. Remember him or her, and don't let anyone else tell you not to.

~ Megan Skaggs ~

I sought the LORD, and he heard me,
and delivered me from all my fears.
The righteous cry, and the LORD heareth,
and delivereth them out of all their troubles.
Psalms 34:4,17

4

Kaylee Louise Dixon

Miscarried on August 25, 2007

My Story:

I went to the hospital because I wasn't feeling well. They told me that I was pregnant! I was so shocked and so happy at the same time! They informed me to take it easy because I had mild cramping. A couple months went by; everything was fine. I heard the heartbeat and saw her on the ultrasound. I was so happy. Then on August 24th I went to bed and had bad dreams about losing the baby. I woke up at around 5 am to find that I was bleeding. I couldn't get a hold of my doctor and I didn't know what to do. I had two other children and never had issues like that before. So I rushed to the hospital. They put me in the room, did an ultrasound and kept asking "are you sure the doctor has seen a heartbeat?" When they asked that my heart dropped. I knew they couldn't see one anymore. They then informed me that I lost the baby. I broke down; I was in shock. They did an exam and told me I could go home and it would pass on its own. It felt like the longest drive home of my life. I laid in bed all day just crying asking God why he would do this to someone. I didn't understand. Around 7 pm I went to dinner to try and get my mind off of it. The whole time I felt like I was having contractions. I went to the bathroom to find myself bleeding really badly. My boyfriend and his parents left the restaurant immediately and took me to the closest hospital. I then was told I would have to have a D&C because the bleeding was so bad. I kept passing out and felt really sick. I had the D&C and woke up and left the hospital.

The hardest thing for me was/is:

Understanding why God took this from me. I still ask every day. When everyone says everything happens for a reason I just can't understand it. And the hardest thing at that point was being on the labor and delivery floor seeing the women having babies and then me leaving after all that without a baby.

Helpful things that family and friends did that I will forever be grateful for:

My boyfriend's mother took me to the doctor for help. She was there for me the whole time and never left my side because I was terrified. They were there for me to just let me cry and that meant a lot.

Things that have helped me cope and deal with the heartache:

I reached out to the people that have had a loss. I think of her every day. I celebrate the time I had being pregnant every year on August 25th.

What I have learned from this:

I have learned to never take anything for granted. Life can go just as quickly as it comes.

How I keep my infant's memory alive:

I had her name put on the memorial wall. I light candles for her. I also wrote her name on a balloon and a message on it then let it go. I put her ultrasound picture in a frame with Precious Moments stickers and hung it on the wall so I can see it every day.

Additional words to help others dealing with the loss of their infant:

Stay strong and positive. You will never get over it like some people told me, but you learn to live with it and cope. You will be able to get through it. And make sure you cry when you feel you need to. When I got home I tried to hide it at first and it was hard. When I let those walls down it was better for me because I was able to grieve.

~ *Crystal Abbott* ~

They Say There is a Reason

They say there is a reason,
They say that time will heal,
But neither time nor reason,
Will change the way I feel,
For no-one knows the heartache,
That lies behind our smiles,
No-one knows how many times,
We have broken down and cried,
We want to tell you something,
So there won't be any doubt,
You're so wonderful to think of,
But so hard to be without.

Author Unknown

5

Hannah Rachelle Ries

February 6, 2007 - February 8, 2007

My Story:

We were excited to be expecting our second child. At our 20-week ultrasound on Friday, September 22nd, the technician asked if my dates could be wrong because the baby was measuring two weeks behind. I knew that my EDD was correct. Other than that, the tech didn't tell us anything, but from that comment we got very concerned. I received a phone call on Monday morning from my nurse practitioner saying that there were issues with the ultrasound and that I should sit down. She said that the baby had only two chambers of the heart (there should have been 4 chambers) and that the baby had Spina Bifida. She also said that she had scheduled us to meet with the Perinatologist the following day to do a more detailed ultrasound. We went to the appointment and learned that these were traits of Trisomy 18. We had the detailed ultrasound to look at the heart and spine more closely. We also saw several cysts in the brain and a two-vessel umbilical cord. It was suggested that I have an amniocentesis to determine for sure if it was T18 and whether it was Full T18, so we decided to go ahead and have it done. We got the results a few days later that it was Full T18 (which means that it was just a fluke and not something that one of us is a carrier for). We also decided to find out the sex of the baby so that we could better plan for the birth/death. We found out that we were going to be having a little girl. We decided to name her Hannah Rachelle. Hannah means God-blessed and Rachelle is my middle name. It was a difficult time because we had no idea if she would make it to term, whether she would be born alive or how long we might have with her in our arms. At 39 weeks, Hannah was breech. I carried Hannah almost 40 weeks (I was due on February 8). Hannah was head-down when she was born so at some point she did flip all on her own - what a good little girl. My labor and delivery was very quick. We got to the hospital at 12:50 am and Hannah was born at 1:11 am on February 6. She weighed 3 lbs., 11.1 ozs. and was 15 1/4 inches long. She had dark blue eyes and dark hair; lots of hair. She was breathing on her own and never needed any help breathing or feeding. We were able to feed her colostrum with a syringe and she always had good color to her skin. Our parents and siblings were with us later that morning when we had professional photos taken of our whole family. I will cherish those pictures of Hannah along with the hundreds of pictures that we took ourselves.

We were able to go home in the evening on the same day that she was born. Hannah never needed any assistance with breathing or anything. It felt so great to be taking home my baby. Doctors didn't think she would even make it to term, much less be born alive!

We spent two, wonderful days with our little girl. Our family got to enjoy her along with us. Her big brother, Logan, didn't know what to think and would only sneak peeks at her through his fingers or from a distance. We had a "birthday party" for our little girl with ice cream cake and a "0" birthday candle; we even sang to her. On the last evening that we had with her, we all went out to eat for dinner. It was the most wonderful feeling to have both of my kids next to each other in the back with their car seats. I will always remember that. Hannah had her eyes open all evening and watched me the whole time we were eating. She was alert all night long and never seemed to shut her eyes to sleep. I should have known that she would die that next morning. Usually babies with Hypoplastic Right or Left Heart Syndrome will only live a couple hours to 48 hours without any intervention, of which Hannah was too small and not strong enough for heart surgery. I was so happy that she was alive and she seemed so strong that I forgot all about that and was hoping that she would live for a week or two. I fed her colostrum with a syringe, since her mouth was so small and she didn't seem strong enough to nurse. She seemed to really like the colostrum. That last night, we finally went to bed at midnight (Hannah was still wide awake, looking around) and I set my alarm for 4 am to feed her and change her. When my alarm went off, it took me a few minutes to fully wake up as I was so tired. I pumped some colostrum for her and then we changed her diaper and dressing. Her eyes were still wide open looking around, but she seemed less responsive than usual. We then fed her with the syringe and she became even less responsive. Sometime during the feeding, she peacefully left us. I didn't notice that she wasn't breathing until we had finished feeding her. She looked so sweet and peaceful. I was expecting her to gasp for air or turn blue because that is what everyone told us would happen, but she never did that. Her heart quit once the PDA valve closed.

Hannah died around 4:30 am on February 8, 2007. She was 51 hours and 19 minutes old. Our strong, spunky little girl lived much longer than anyone thought that she would.

We held her until late morning when we called everyone to let them know. We had a memorial service for her on Saturday and did a balloon release. Everyone wrote a message to her on the pink balloons and we released them to Heaven. We had her cremated since we have no idea where we will live in the future and none of our family is in town. We put her ashes in a heart-shaped urn engraved with: *Hannah Rachelle 2/6/07 - 2/8/07 Sweet Little Girl.* My husband and I have pendant necklaces with some of her ashes to wear around our necks all the time. I will cherish the time that we had with her and am grateful that she was such a strong-willed little girl and fought hard to meet and spend time with her family.

The hardest thing for me was/is:

Knowing that she was going to die and there was nothing that I could do. I wanted so much to be able to save her, but I couldn't. It's hard to imagine what she would look like or be doing today and how her big brother would be playing with her if she was here.

Helpful things that family and friends did that I will forever be grateful for:

A friend of ours had a lady come to our home and do hand and foot casts of Hannah and all of our hands for a collage. I never would have thought to do that so I'm forever grateful to Valeri for doing that for us; she even paid for it.

Things that have helped me cope and deal with the heartache:

Having lots of pictures of Hannah and having more children, but they will never replace her.

What I have learned from this:

We may not know God's plan, but there is a reason for things that happen. I lost another baby, in the first trimester and then went on to have three, healthy babies;

triplets! I would not have my triplets if I had my other two babies here on Earth.

How I keep my infant's memory alive:

I have pictures of her in my house, talk about her with my family and friends and think of her often.

Additional words to help others dealing with the loss of their infant:

You will never forget your baby, but you can be happy again. I always like to remember that both my little girls are waiting in Heaven for me.

~ Kristin Rachelle Ries ~

And God shall wipe away all tears from their eyes; and there shall be no more death, neither sorrow, nor crying, neither shall there be any more pain: for the former things are passed away.

Revelation 21:4

6

Andrew Kevin Costa

February 20, 2000

My Story:

I was 40-weeks pregnant with a great pregnancy. I had a scheduled C-section on February 18, 2000. I went in at 6 am and found out there was a problem with my blood work and I was going to be transferred to a bigger hospital that specializes in high risk. In the ambulance on my way to the hospital I started to have contractions. I arrived at the hospital and the doctor tried to stop the contractions but nothing was working. I found out that the problem with my blood was that I had no platelets, which is what is needed to make your blood clot. I couldn't have surgery or deliver him because they were afraid I would bleed to death. I was put on steroids and platelet transfusions hoping my counts would increase enough to deliver. As I waited I ended up catching group A strep from someone else in the hospital. Things just got worse from there. I went into respiratory arrest a few times and the contractions still being really strong something had to be done. Finally, 48 hours later my counts were just high enough and he was starting to come one way or another. I was brought into the OR and put under general anesthesia for my C-section. I had just seen my son on an ultrasound before I went into surgery. I woke up one week later. I was in an induced coma so my body could heal from the infection I caught. As I woke up I was looking for my son and I was told he had passed during the surgery. They are not exactly sure why either; too much stress after all that time or because he was so far down and needed to be pulled up for the section. My husband was left to make a lot of the decisions because I was in a coma, but they said they worked on my son for a long time to get him back, but he never took a breath. This is the hardest thing I have ever had to go through in my life.

The hardest thing for me was/is:

The hardest part was not being able to see my son right after he was born. When I saw him one week later, they had already done an autopsy and I wasn't really able to unwrap him from the blanket or anything. I have great support in my family and my husband. I just could never understand how I was going to keep myself going.

Helpful things that family and friends did that I will forever be grateful for:

My family was great and they still are. They talk about him and treat him as if he was real. A lot of people don't do that. They let me talk and never tell me to get over it.

Things that have helped me cope and deal with the heartache:

I found a great support group at my local hospital that I attend every month. All of us there are very close and we always know we can call anyone of these people anytime we need to. That has probably been the best thing I ever did. These are people that understand you and will never judge how you are feeling.

What I have learned from this:

I have learned a lot. I have learned that I need to feel whatever I want and not let others dictate my grief.

How I keep my infant's memory alive:

I talk about him just like any other child. I included him when people ask me how many children I have and we celebrate his birthday with a balloon release and attend memorial walks. I have his picture on my mantle.

Additional words to help others dealing with the loss of their infant:

My advice is to take your time. Don't rush your grief. You need to go through the motions of it all and never let anyone tell you when it has been long enough or how you should feel.

~ Maureen Costa ~

7

Amber Lynn Costa

April 30, 2009

My Story:

I found out I was pregnant by surprise; it wasn't expected. My husband and I were so happy though. I had had some issues with diabetes during the first few months, but things were getting under control. Having had a stillborn 10 years ago I was very scared and nervous. Every time I went to the doctor, I was afraid something was wrong. I had an ultrasound at 16 weeks and we found out we were having a girl. I was so excited since I have had three boys. Everything was perfect. I had a really bad feeling one day before my appointment and when I got in the office I started to cry and told the doctor I thought something was wrong and was afraid she wasn't going to find a heartbeat. I had had a dream the night before. The doctor assured me I was just panicking and we continued with the appointment. She tried to find the heartbeat with the doppler, but had no luck. She said she was going to do an ultrasound to get a better look. As she was doing the ultrasound I could just see in her face something was wrong. She looked at me and told me that there was no heartbeat. I thought I was going to die. I was by myself because I told my husband it was just a regular appointment and he didn't have to come. After I found out, she told me I had to be induced and deliver her. I was in complete shock. I had three previous C-sections so having to be induced scared me too. I was sent over to the hospital where we started the process. My husband came right away and I could see the hurt in his face; he was devastated. After 10 hours of contractions, my little girl was born at 18 weeks. She was so tiny. We had her baptized and the nurses took some pictures for us. We had her cremated and she is home with us now. I just couldn't believe what had happen. Now months later I feel I am still in a bit of shock and disbelief.

The hardest thing for me was/is:

The hardest thing for me was my sister and sister-in-law were both pregnant and each due three days after me. I had to go through their whole pregnancy; watching them grow bigger and then deliver their beautiful babies. I love my nephews to death, but it is so hard to see and be around. I am just moving slowly and on my terms right now helping myself try to heal.

Helpful things that family and friends did that I will forever be grateful for:

My family was great and they talk about her all the time. They understand when I can't go to certain things because it is still too hard for me and they don't judge.

Things that have helped me cope and deal with the heartache:

I just remember my baby as much as I can. I have pictures and her clothes and hat from the hospital.

What I have learned from this:

I am learning to take things slow and take things minute-by-minute. Then hour-by-hour and do what I need to do for me to move forward. I will never forget my angels no matter what people think or say.

How I keep my infant's memory alive:

I have my daughter's picture and clothing from the hospital. I also have a tattoo of her tiny footprints. I will always talk about her; she was my child whether people accept it or not.

Additional words to help others dealing with the loss of their infant:

My advice is to take your time. Don't rush your grief. You need to go through the motions of it all and never let anyone tell you when it has been long enough or how you should feel.

~ Maureen Costa ~

While we look not at the things which are seen, but at the things which are not seen: for the things which are seen are temporal; but the things which are not seen are eternal.

2 Corinthians 4:18

8

Ivy Chyme Lucas

March 8, 2005 - March 8, 2005

My Story:

My husband and I were married on May 23, 2004. On our honeymoon in Maui we were adamant about being ready for our first baby. We were together seven years and ready. Our first try we were pregnant...lucky I guess. The pregnancy was amazing. I loved it. I had perfect appointments; everything was on track. No need for tests or checking, everything seemed to be normal. I don't even remember her original due date, but we chose to not find out the sex before hand. Our first baby; a complete surprise.

I woke up at 5 am in the morning on March 8th, ecstatic because I *knew* I was having 3-to-5 minute contractions. I woke up my husband and we scrambled and headed to the hospital. We were *so* excited our baby would arrive soon.

When we arrived at the hospital, we checked in and got to a side room to be monitored. After a couple of tries the nurse couldn't find the baby's heartbeat. I felt something was wrong. What was supposed to be the best day of our lives became a miserable, long, horrible day. After a few more tries she says "We aren't finding a heartbeat." I was numb and my husband just as shocked. Labor had started so they refused to do a C-section. I was in labor until 5:25 that afternoon with huge contractions; all day knowing I was giving *birth* to my dead baby.

When the time arrived I gave birth to a beautiful baby girl. We named her Ivy Chyme. She was 7 lbs., 11 ozs. and 23-inches long with dark brown hair, long fingernails, and seemed perfect. Paul cut the umbilical cord. Everything a normal pregnancy would entail...except instead of crying it was silent and I kept waiting, just hoping it was a mistake and she would open her eyes. We both held her and cried and cried and cried. The hospital took her away after awhile, but during that special time we had our pictures taken with her and got all of the papers for a birth/death certificate, footprints, a lock of hair and plaster molds of her two hands and one foot. She was perfect and we could not understand why this had happened. My world had ended; I felt empty, alone and so did my husband, but we couldn't connect on any level to deal with the situation. We made split decisions. We chose to have her cremated and never had any service or ceremony. We weren't into that. We actually waited to drive to each of our parent's houses; empty handed and cried about our answer to "where's the baby?" I will never forget her. I have a tattoo of her name and birth date on my left shoulder, surrounded by Ivy leaves. I connected with this site angelbabies.com and just found a place to connect with other people who had suffered child loss. I just read a lot at first, but then started talking about it and am glad that something good in the way of sharing can help others in dealing with the loss.

The hardest thing for me was/is:

Going home with no baby and explaining to people what happened without feeling guilty or empty. It was hard to pick up and go back to life. Life didn't stop just because we had a loss. The other thing that was difficult was that it put a huge barrier in my relationship with my husband for the year after. We did make it through.

Helpful things that family and friends did that I will forever be grateful for:

When the time was right we talk about Ivy with family. My father is an avid fisherman; it's his passion. His boat is named *Ivy Chyme.* He asked our permission and it's a calming thing to see. It makes me know that they were hurt too, but wanted to remember Ivy just as I did; that it wasn't just going to be forgotten or me being shamed. After a time, my mother-in-law had a pink elephant at her house...she told me she bought it for Ivy. The little things help. Not too overwhelming just when it was time.

Things that have helped me cope and deal with the heartache:

We had another child right after we lost Ivy and it was a trying pregnancy. We learned after three months that Ivy had mosaicism with her chromosomes. Somehow she managed to make the full pregnancy with no signs of trouble at all. I write about her, I have pictures, and I remind Tyler that he has a sister named Ivy. I still include her in my thoughts of our "family."

A lot of people came to me that had losses of all kinds and unfortunately it is more common than we think, but no one ever talks about it before the birth.

What I have learned from this:

I take every day and live it to the most because our life time can be years, days, or for Ivy, just the time I had with her inside me. I take lots of pictures, I have a great and supportive family that I have grown to love every single one, in-laws and all because the moments we have are what we can have right now. Life is not a guarantee; cherish it.

How I keep my infant's memory alive:

I talk about her with my son as she is part of our family. I have a stuffed, giraffe toy that my husband put a diaper on to practice with. It was his first newborn diaper before Ivy was stillborn. I keep that on my night stand and everyone, even my three-year-old knows it's Ivy's giraffe.

Additional words to help others dealing with the loss of their infant:

Take the time *you* need to recover and understand. Cry when you need to cry, don't be sorry for it. Take a grain of salt with comments people will make because no one understands the situation as another mother or father who has lost their child.

~ Paul and Kim Lucas ~

Rest Gently With Me

Startled and fascinated by the beauty and fragility
of your wings, I watch as you move
so gently
so quietly
almost unexpectedly
through my world.
And then I watch as you move on,
fluttering softly into the distance.
Pleading silently, I beg you,
please ... don't go.
I haven't yet had the time
to memorize
to remember
to understand
the uniqueness of the beauty that is yours.
I know I cannot hold you for long,
capturing you for my world.
But, rest gently with me
if only for a moment.
That I may treasure the memory
and the beauty of the
gift that you are.

Author unknown

9

Angel Elizabeth Denniston

December 18, 2007 is when I found out there was no heartbeat. I lost her at home in my shower three days later, December 21, 2007.

My Story:

I found out I was pregnant the weekend before Thanksgiving, 2007. I was scared. Financially I was not in a good place to be having another baby. Angel was my fifth and emotionally, life was not any better. However with each day that passed, I fell more and more in love with this tiny, little being.

I went for my ultrasound on December 18. My mom went with me as Angel's father and I were not doing well and he gave no support at that time. I was anxious at the thought of seeing my baby for the first time and hearing the swishing of the heartbeat. Instead there was silence. No movement; no pounding of the baby's heartbeat. Just a tiny oblong image of what was my baby. The ultrasound technician left the room for what seemed like an eternity. Later, one of the midwives came in and spoke to me. She didn't want me giving up hope yet, so she sent me to the lab for blood work and I was supposed to have more done two days later with a follow up appointment to be scheduled for two weeks. I never made it to the second blood draw. I began spotting the morning I was supposed to go in for a draw. I called the clinic and left a message for the midwife who had seen me two days prior. She was not there. I received a call back from one of the physicians who informed me nicely, but clinically, that I should have been told a miscarriage was imminent since a heartbeat wasn't detected. He told me what to look for and what to expect. When I asked about coming into the clinic he replied, “No, you can take care of it right there at home.” The next morning I woke up to the heaviest bleeding I'd ever experienced. I cleaned myself up the best I could, changed my shirt and panties, layed a towel down on the couch. I'd bled through everything and tried to rest. 90 minutes later the bleeding was worse and I decided to try and take a shower. I had already passed an enormous amount of clots and the bleeding wouldn't stop. I remember closing my eyes and leaning into the shower wall. I felt a slight pressure and five minutes later, what there was of my baby slipped from me.

The hardest thing for me was/is:

There were several things. For one, what there was of my baby covered my shower drain and while I couldn't make out everything, I saw little hands. My doctor told me there was no way possible that I could have...the baby had stopped developing at six weeks so technically (according to him) there really was no baby. Do I believe it? No. I didn't then and I never will. The other thing was that most of my baby's remains were washed down the drain. There was no service, no burial, no marker. It's been rather tough dealing with that.

Helpful things that family and friends did that I will forever be grateful for:

I think my oldest son, who was 13 at the time, really deserves a hero's award. That young man pitched in with chores when I was healing physically. He helped to entertain his siblings so that I could try and rest. And when he heard me crying my heart out, he put his arms around me and cried along with me. He's 15 now and I couldn't ask for a finer young man!

Things that have helped me cope and deal with the heartache:

First of all, I named my baby Angel, after my great-grandmother and Elizabeth for her aunt that died before her first birthday. Then I made a memory box which contains poems, family pictures, my pregnancy tests and special little mementos of what could have been. I made a collage for my wall. I have several bears that were given to me through various websites that donate bears to grieving parents. One I purchased is pretty well beat up because it has gone everywhere with me, even to work and when the pain would get to be too much to deal with I'd hold that little bear as tight as I could.

What I have learned from this:

Life is fragile and can be lost at any time. Death is no respecter of persons, but one thing that death can never do is stop me from being Angel's momma. We are temporarily separated; we are forever mother and child.

How I keep my infant's memory alive:

I made an online memorial where I would post poems and letters that I'd written at different stages of my grief. Finally I got a memorial tattoo on my right shoulder of an angel baby asleep in the hands of God. Since she can't be in my hands right now, there are no better hands for her to be in than God's.

Additional words to help others dealing with the loss of their infant:

It's okay to grieve and it's also okay to feel those moments of joy because there will be both. When you need to grieve, grieve; let the tears flow and don't hold them back for the sake of anyone. When you feel joy and laughter, embrace it and let it happen. It doesn't mean you've forgotten your teeny one. It's actually just the opposite. You will never forget, but you will heal. You will heal only after you have grieved long enough for you!

~ Lorelei ~

And the ransomed of the LORD shall return,
and come to Zion with songs and
everlasting joy upon their heads:
they shall obtain joy and gladness,
and sorrow and sighing shall flee away.

Isaiah 35:10

10

Michael John Andrade

January 14, 2009

My Story:

I have three boys who were born without too many issues with pregnancy. I started a new relationship and he had no children. We made the decision to try and have a baby together, as we had been together for almost five years. I went off my birth control and it took a year to get pregnant. At six weeks I lost that child and subsequently became pregnant again and I again lost that child at eight weeks. Three months later I was pregnant again and with much anxiety waited for the first three months to pass, and they did. I was so overjoyed that I was going to be able to carry this baby to term. I didn't have many issues with pregnancy other than I had very little weight gain. I gained a total of 10 pounds. In my last month I was going for weekly stress tests to monitor him since I had not gained any weight. We found out it was a boy since I was 39 at the time and we had an amnio done. We passed with flying colors; another milestone passed. At 34 weeks

I went in for a routine stress test without a worry in the world. I was just anxious getting down to the wire. I went by myself as I had been through these numerous times and had no issues. The nurse proceeded to try and locate our son and could not find a heartbeat. She then, without any hesitation said: let's take you over to ultrasound and mark him since he may be hiding. We took the walk across the hall and at this point I am getting a little worried, but not overly so. I laid down on the bed and the technician started to find the heartbeat. 30 seconds later, he walked out of the room and the nurse walked back in and said they were calling my doctor. At that point I asked with a very heavy heart (in more of a statement than a question) "there is no heart beat is there" and she said no. At that point all my dreams for Michael and all the hope just flashed in my head and I cried and cried.

The nurses were fantastic and emptied the area immediately and took me back over to the stress-testing area so that I could call my partner. I tried calling my partner, whom I could not get a hold of. I then called my mom at work and she asked what was wrong. I broke down again and told her they didn't find a heartbeat. She left work immediately and showed up at the hospital 20 minutes later with my dad. At that point something happened and I felt a huge gush; I knew I was losing our son. They immediately started to prep me for a C-section. It became obvious to everyone I was starting to hemorrhage. My dad at this point was still trying to get a hold of my partner, whom still was not picking up the phone. I was begging them to wait until my partner got there before anything was done, but it was an emergency and they couldn't wait. My mom ended up coming into the room with me; thank God for my mom. She was my rock during all of this. I had asked my mom, "Please don't let them take anything out." I still, at this point, was trying to think of the future for my partner who has not had any children.

I was taken into recovery, almost numb at this point and the nurse asked me if I would like to see my baby. Everything else was a blur except for that moment. During my C-section my partner had arrived and was told the news our son didn't make it. He was by my bed when they brought our son to us. I held him and he was perfect, my partner could not bring himself to hold him. I uncovered him and looked at his fingers and toes; amazingly even in that moment, you still check to make sure all fingers and toes are still there. I looked at our son and felt something just give inside me, a dam burst and it was just uncontrollable. I had them take our son at this point.

The nurses made sure I had a room as far from the nursery as possible and put butterflies on my door. I later found out what butterflies signified. Later that day people started to call and come by and I just couldn't bring myself to show emotion to any of them, it felt like my own private hell. The social worker came to see me multiple times, but I refused to see her. It was like I didn't want to give any more to anyone after what had just happened. Then it was brought up what to do with Michael. My first response was, I want nothing done I want it *all* to go away like having a ceremony would make it all too real. I wasn't at all prepared to go to the hospital and think of how to put my son to rest. I went to the hospital to have a baby. How could I ever leave here without a baby in my arms? My mom was the person who convinced me that I needed to do something. I relented and asked could we make it very small. I didn't even know anything about putting someone to rest or making arrangements; let alone how to do that to my son who I had just birthed. Nothing in life prepares you for that. My mom did everything for me. She made the arrangements with my blessing on everything; she was wonderful as was my dad.

The hardest thing for me was/is:

Leaving the hospital was probably one of the hardest things to do. I had to walk by the nursery with all those babies and watch other moms leaving with their babies. I cried as I left that day, not knowing what the future would bring. Just knowing I was leaving something of myself behind that day.

What I have learned from this:

I have learned that you never know what life is going to throw at you and what you think you are least prepared for, in reality you are. Time is always a healer, it doesn't ever make you forget the love and the pain you feel for your child, but it helps you get through each and every day.

How I keep my infant's memory alive:

I have really struggled with how to keep Michael alive. This year would have been his first Christmas. I put a blue butterfly on the tree so that in spirit he is still there with us. I asked my partner to give me a locket with his picture engraved on it for Christmas so that he is always near my heart and always in it. The day of his birth/death is approaching and I am not sure how I am going to deal with that day, but at the very least I plan on releasing 34 blue balloons as that is how many weeks he was.

Additional words to help others dealing with the loss of their infant:

There really are no words to help another grieving parent. Nothing people can say can ease that pain or loss. I am still learning how to cope and I think in years to come I will still be learning.

~ Nicky Craig ~

Message from heaven

I am not so far from you,
Just a little way beyond;
Past the cares and past the pain,
Far past my earthly bonds.
When you feel you miss me most,
As years go drifting by;
Each memory will prove to you,
That our love will never die.
For memories are but a touch,
From the Father's gentle hand;
To heal your pain and mend your hearts,
To help you understand...
That while I left you far too soon,
I did not leave alone;
For the Father sent His angels,
To gently take me home.
Take comfort when you think of me,
Keep my love alive in your heart;
And with the warmth of each memory,
We will never be apart.

Author Unknown

On March 11, my husband and I went to go find out the sex of the baby. When she said it was a boy I felt a little sad because I wanted a girl since I had two boys, but I was happy too that everything was fine and he was doing good. All my appointments were good; the heart-beat always strong. I never expected anything to go wrong, but on April 3rd everything changed. That morning was normal. I took my son to school and picked him up. Later we all went to see a football game then got back home. Around 6 pm, my belly started hurting. I was five-months along and I thought it was nothing and that it would go away in a while. We decided to go out and eat and while we were there the pain started to feel like contractions so we left and I called my doctor, but he wasn't in and the one on-call told me to lie on my left side and if in two hours I still had the pain to go to the ER. Well, I fell asleep and when I woke up it was past 10 pm and the pain wasn't as bad so I got up to go pee and while I was in the restroom, still sitting in the toilet, I blew my nose and I just felt a gush of water come out. When I wiped there was blood and I just knew my water broke so I told my husband, who then rushed me to the hospital. I was admitted and they confirmed that the water had broken. They checked the baby's heartbeat and it was strong; he was fine. The following day they did a test to see how much fluid I had left. They said it was a little bit and that even though I kept producing it, it would still be leaking out. I stayed in the hospital for many days, where they monitored me for infection and the baby's heartbeat every 30 minutes; and always his heart was strong which would give me hope that he was going to make it. Well on the 10th, the on-call doctor decided to send me home where I would still need to be on complete bed rest, take the antibiotics and check for fever. On the 11th, in the morning I went to go pee again and this time when I wiped it felt weird, so I wiped again and this time something came out. My husband was at work and my mother-in-law was there with me so I told her to take me to the hospital, but she said "no" that we should call the ambulance so we did. While I was on the phone with them they made me get on my hands and knees until they got there. Then they took my pants off to see what was going on and they told me that I had a prolapsed cord so I was rushed to the hospital. They had to keep it moist and kept checking to make sure it had a pulse which it did. I wanted them to take me to the hospital I had left from, but they said another one was closer and the sooner I got there the better chances my baby had so I told them to take me to that one. When we got there they checked to see if I was dilated, which I was but only two centimeters. After they were done checking me, they went on to tell me there was nothing they could do to save him because I was only 23-weeks along and I needed to be 24 weeks for them to at least try; his lungs were just not developed enough. They said that within four hours he would pass away and then they would induce me. It actually took longer for them to get me into a room. While I was waiting, my mother got there, as well as my sister, brother-in-law and his wife. My husband had gotten there too after we had called him. The nurses were so nice; they were letting everyone be in the room with me. When I finally got a room, I was induced and then it took me almost 24 hours to give birth because I was just not dilating. While I was pushing he came out, feet-first and then the cervix closed on his tiny head and he stayed like that for about four more hours. My cervix just wouldn't open. Finally, I got this very hard contraction and he came out completely, but there wasn't anyone in there to catch him. So the nurse came in and got him, put him on my chest and I couldn't believe how little he was, but still so perfect with all ten, tiny fingers and ten, tiny toes and just hoping to hear him cry, but the cry never came and now I had to make arrangements for a funeral. The nurse took many pictures for us with the baby which we named Emmanuel. He was born at 2:50 pm on the 12th of April and weighted 1lb., and 3ozs. I had so much family show up there, and just be there with me. My brother-in-law and I planned the funeral and I will never be able to thank him enough for all his help because without it I have no idea what I would have done. My husband helped too but my brother in law did most of the decision making with my blessing.

The hardest thing for me was/is:

The hardest thing for me was, and is still, letting go of the guilt; that maybe I didn't do enough to save him. Seeing him in that tiny casket and knowing that it was going to be the last time I got to see his little body. But I know that one day I will get to see and hold him again.

Helpful things family and friends did that I will forever be grateful for:

I will forever be grateful for the emotional support. They were there and willing to listen to me and help me out with my other two kids when I just couldn't get out of bed. They were doing everything they could to help me out and I thank them so much for that.

Things that have helped me cope and deal with the heartache:

What has helped me the most is music. I now listen to KLOV radio and the songs they play are just so amazing. They touched my heart and every time I would get in the car I would hear a song that would lift my spirit up more and give me hope. It seemed like the right song was always on when I needed it.

What I have learned from this:

I have learned to never take anything for granted and just live life a day at a time. That time really does help you heal; not forget, but makes the pain less intense. That even though I don't have Emmanuel next to me, I still love him and won't ever forget about him, and no matter what people say or think I am a mother of three, not two.

How I keep my infant's memory alive:

The way I keep Emmanuel alive. I have a necklace with an angel and his name and day he was born that I always wear. I have a picture of his little feet on my cell. I talk about him to his brothers and I'm planning on getting a tattoo on my left wrist of an angel and his name above it. I haven't gotten it done yet because I'm a chicken for pain.

Additional words to help others dealing with the loss of an infant:

Grieve at your own pace and I don't really know what else to say because nothing I say will make it any better for some one that just lost a baby.

~ Patricia Garcia ~

I waited patiently for the LORD;
and he inclined unto me,
and heard my cry.

Psalms 40:1

12

Lauren Elizabeth Welling

Stillborn June 1, 2007

My story:

My husband and I had one daughter and had waited for awhile to try again because I was trying to get rid of a uterine fibroid naturally. So, we were so excited when we found out that I was pregnant. At the time, Kristen was a little 4-year-old. We found out it was a girl and we were all so happy. We couldn't wait to have another little girl! I had a C-section with my first daughter, but was very anxious to try for a VBAC for this baby. We found a place, four-or-so hours away from our home that would help us with this goal. My husband and I took an awesome Bradley Childbirth class and had planned on using the wonderful doula who had taught it. We are a family with a strong faith in God and we were just certain that everything was going to go well. Towards the end of the pregnancy, which had no complications, I had gone for a doctor's appointment on a Wednesday. A friend took me as I was so miserable and could barely walk anymore because of back pain. The midwife had used an old ultrasound machine to just check the position of the baby and found that she was feet down. I was so upset about that. Then she asked me about her movements, and I just said she hasn't been moving as much. The midwife asked me if I wanted to stay and check things out on the fetal monitor and I declined. I feel in my heart that was my fateful decision. It was a long trip home and I was exhausted. Well, the next day I was worried about the breech position and made many phone calls and some appointments to try to get Lauren turned. I noticed later that afternoon that she wasn't moving much and later that night when my husband arrived home, I shared my concerns. He wanted me to go to the emergency room at 11 pm that night, but I thought I could still feel her movements. We went to the clinic the next day and the PA and nurse couldn't find the heartbeat. It took them forever to figure this out! Finally they sent me to a bigger hospital with an ultrasound and the horrible truth came crashing down on us. After this heartbreaking news, we prayed about where to go for the delivery, and felt the Lord told us to go to another town with a larger hospital for a C-section. I am so glad we went there. They knew how to deal with infant loss pretty well and a professional photographer came and took pictures. It was the saddest day of my life. I felt totally abandoned by God and so heartbroken.

My faith was shaken to the core. We buried her a week later in a small graveside service with family and friends around.

The hardest part for me:

I had such faith that things would work out, I felt so completely betrayed by God.

Helpful things from family and friends:

When we got home from the hospital, our house was totally cleaned and the yard completely manicured. A friend had put vases of fresh, white daisies everywhere and planted my deck pots with some of my favorite flowers.

Things that have helped me cope and deal with the heartache:

I took a Grief Share class. My faith in God has slowly been rebuilt and I have recognized that God was not punishing me or abandoning me, but that He weeps right alongside me and gives me the strength to make it through.

I also have a gold, heart necklace with her footprints engraved on it, and this especially gave me comfort around my first Christmas without her.

I read a book called *Heaven* by Randy Alcorn. This helped me to have a better viewpoint on what heaven will be like.

I have learned:

To be compassionate to those who have lost children or have lost other close family members too. I have learned that I can live through a terrible experience and I guess, how to grieve normally.

How I keep my infant's memory alive:

We talk about Lauren and we have a picture of her up in our bedroom. We have a beautiful angel statue with her name on it that some nice friends gave us and we celebrate her birthday with letting balloons go by her grave.

Additional words:

I still miss my daughter and always will. I know that I will be reunited with her again someday in heaven and this had made heaven so much more real to me. God will give you the strength to cope and deal with your loss. Your heart will heal and you will learn to live life in a new state of *normal*. Don't give up hope.

~ *Suzanne (Olson) Welling* ~

Gone Too Soon

This was a life that hardly begun
no time to find your place in the sun
no time to do all you could have done
but we loved you enough for a lifetime
No time to enjoy the world and its wealth
No time to take life down off the shelf
no time to sing the song of yourself
though you had enough love for a lifetime
Those who live long endure sadness and tears
but you'll never suffer the sorrowing years
no betrayal, no anger
no hatred, no fears
Just love, only love in your lifetime..
Author Unknown

13

Travis Ernest Gaouette

Born/passed February 12, 2008

My Story:

I found out I was pregnant with Travis in October of 2007. We were very surprised, but also very excited. My son Trevor, who was three at the time, was thrilled to know he was going to be a big brother. When I was about six-weeks along, I started spotting a little though it was brown. I went to the emergency room and they checked me over and said everything was okay; that the brown meant it was 'old blood' and probably just my body adjusting to the pregnancy. As time went on, the spotting never really stopped, but wasn't constant so I kept my Ob-Gyn updated and continued on. While I kept being told everything was okay I had a nagging feeling that something was wrong. Every few weeks something inside me would gnaw at me to go to the hospital and every time they would do an ultrasound and would say everything was okay. Around Thanksgiving I noticed the spotting was starting to get more frequent and redder. Still the emergency room trips would be the same; everything is okay. On January 3rd, I started bleeding heavily and now started to have incredible cramps. Again the answer was the same, except my doctor took me out of work as a precaution and told me not to be on my feet for too long a time. My son turned four on January 18 and we had a small party for him. I didn't want him to miss out on that even though I was having problems. Later on that evening after the party I was rushed to the hospital because I was in so much pain I couldn't move. Besides the bleeding and cramping, I was now starting to have a very tender pain on the upper-right side of my abdomen and started passing blood clots. After being thoroughly checked in the hospital, the doctors couldn't come to any conclusions as to what was going on. I was sent home and told to stay off my feet as much as possible.

On February 8, everything changed. I was once again rushed to the hospital because of bleeding and pain. This time they found what was wrong. I had placenta abruption, a premature separation of the placenta to the uterine wall. It usually happens in the third trimester and less than five percent of pregnancies actually experience it. It can be hard to diagnosis due the positioning of the baby. Whenever I had an ultrasound Travis was blocking the placenta so it was never seen. I was then admitted to the hospital. The doctors thought that I would have to be induced because the situation had become life-threatening with all the blood loss, and I had to be given quite a bit of blood to make up for it. I was devastated. Suddenly, the next morning the bleeding stopped. It was a very good sign and my doctors were becoming hopeful that I would be able to hang on to the pregnancy for at least the next two weeks, which would put me at 24 weeks. After a couple more days of being monitored on the delivery floor, I was moved to the high-risk floor. I became very hopeful at this point. A few hours later my world came crashing down. I started bleeding more than I ever had and started having contractions. I was moved back down to the delivery floor and tried to prepare myself for what was about to happen. At 4:35 am on February 12, my son Travis Ernest was born. He passed away at 4:45 am. There was a priest at the hospital who baptized him immediately. I was able to hold him and say good-bye to him. I kissed him, told him I loved him and that I was sorry. The next few hours were basically a blur for me. My doctor wanted me to stay in the hospital overnight, but I refused. I just wanted to get home and be with my family.

Two days later we had his funeral and after it was over I felt at peace. I knew he was okay. One year after I lost Travis, I found out I was pregnant again. In October of 2009 I had my baby girl Amber. I know that Travis watched over me during my pregnancy with her and that he is my family's guardian angel; forever watching over his family.

The hardest thing for me was/is:

One of the hardest things for me was to tell my son that his brother went to heaven. Trevor was upset about it, but took it very well. He understood what happened and accepted it. The other thing that was very hard for me was accepting the fact that it wasn't my fault what happened. I kept thinking what could I have done differently that could have changed the outcome. I blamed myself for what happened. I kept thinking that I'm his mom and I should have been able to keep him safe. Finally I did accept the truth that I did everything I could for Travis. The truth was what happened to me couldn't have been prevented. It was just one of the things that can happen during pregnancy.

Helpful things from family and friends:

My grandparents and my Aunt Joyce did some of the most helpful things for me during this time. My grandparents offered to have him buried on their plot, which I immediately accepted. It helped me get some peace knowing he would be surrounded by family and wouldn't be alone. My aunt did all of the planning for the service; she knew that I wouldn't be able to do it. She wouldn't make any decisions for it without asking me what I wanted, but once she got my answers she took care of the rest. She also helped me come up with Ernest for his middle name. I couldn't think of what to give him for a middle name so she suggested naming him after his great-grandfather (my dad's father.) I adored him and he passed away many years ago. I know he would have very happy to have Travis named after him. Coincidently my grandfather is buried at the same cemetery very close to Travis. Without the help of my grandparents and my aunt I don't know what I would have done.

What I have learned from this:

I have learned to not take anything for granted anymore. I have also learned to let go of so many things that I have held onto. I have accepted that things happen for a reason though you may not know what that reason is.

How I keep my infant's memory alive:

I keep his memory alive by thinking about him every day. I have two different necklaces that symbolize him; one is an angel given to me on the day we buried him and another is a little charm baby with his birth stone as the belly. The hospital gave me a beautiful box that has his blanket, hat and other items of his. It also contains a little photo album with pictures the nurses took of him wrapped up and with his hat on and his foot prints on the cover. I also go to the cemetery when I can. I know I'm also keeping his memory alive by telling my story and hoping to let others who are going through this know that I understand the pain.

Additional words:

The pain will never go away, but will lessen with time. You will never get over what happened, but will learn to deal with it. And don't feel guilty when you find yourself laughing or happy. I did feel guilty when that first happened, but then I realized that I was starting to heal.

~ Crystal Gaouette ~

For I will turn their mourning into joy,
and will comfort them,
and make them rejoice from their sorrow.

Jeremiah 31:13

14

Seth Ryan Pumphrey

April 16, 2009
(11 wonderful hours)

My Story:

We found out that we were expecting our second child in September of 2008, and we were very excited. In December, we found out that our little girl would soon have a little brother. That day the doctor told us that something *might* be wrong with our little boy. On December 18th we found out that our little Seth Ryan had a rare, but fatal NTD called anencephaly via a level II ultrasound. Up until that day, I had never heard of this condition. The doctor told us that a baby could not live outside of the womb with this condition, and if he made it to delivery, he would only live minutes or if lucky, days, because with anencephaly, the baby lacks most of his brain. We were devastated. We chose, without any doubt, to carry to term. We knew that it was the best thing to do not only for us, but for our unborn son also. I was due on May 15th, but had a C-Section at 36 weeks, on April 16. Seth Ryan lived for 11 wonderful hours on earth.

The hardest thing for me was/is:

Seeing other babies that are the same age that Seth should be.

Helpful things that family and friends did that I will forever be grateful for:

They supported me 100 percent through everything!

Things that have helped me cope and deal with the heartache:

Doing things to help keep his memory alive, but most of all, his big sister helped me cope the most!

What I have learned from this:

Life is too short to take for granted, and to be aware of all possible things that could happen during pregnancy.

How I keep my infant's memory alive:

We talk about him *every* day with his 2-year-old sister, and look at pictures often.

Additional words to help others dealing with the loss of their infant:

Trust God, and *He* will get you through! And don't be afraid to ask for help if you need it. Grieving is different for everyone, so take your time!

~ PJ Pumphrey ~

Because of You

Because of you I appreciate
the sunset more than before.
Because of you I stop to look up at
the moon and wish upon a star.
Because of you I look forward to
hearing the birds sing in the morning,
and thank God for their beautiful songs.
Because of you I am more understanding of others and
accept people for who they are.
Because of you material things do not matter.
Because of you the touch of someone you love is more
precious than any gift you can receive.
Because of you I have a broken heart
but I thank God for sending you to me.
For there is no stronger love than I hold for you.
Until we meet again...

Author Unknown

15

Madison Abigail Paqueo

September 24, 2008 - October 20, 2008

My Story:

My daughter's name was Madison Abigail Paqueo, and she was a miracle baby.

I went in at 10 weeks for my first prenatal doctor's appointment. When they tried to find her heartbeat there wasn't one. They assumed they were too early in trying to find it, so they decided I should come back two weeks later.

At 12 weeks, the doctor could not find a heart beat still. They set up for an immediate ultrasound. And as soon as they set everything up, there she was. She was so full of energy and movement, I had no concerns. However the doctors still could not get a number for the BPM. After several ultrasounds that day, they finally came up with a BPM of 59.

A month later I was sent to another doctor. After about two hours, the ultrasound was done and the doctors told us that they found several issues. She had a short nose bone, thickening on the neck and, of course, the extremely low heartbeat. They suggested an amnio; he said he believed it was Down's syndrome. After two, long weeks and a ton of research on Down's babies, they called and informed us that all chromosomes were as they should be and according to their charts she was normal.

Less than 48 hours later, I was sent to my third doctor. He did an echocardiogram and gave me the diagnosis I was not ready to hear. Madison was diagnosed with Atrio-Ventricular Septal Defect. She had only three chambers; one atrium and two ventricles, with one central opening instead of two separate. Her natural pacemaker did not work and she had arrhythmia. On top of all this, they diagnosed her with Sidus Adversus; her stomach and liver were not in their correct places in her body. She also had a third-degree heart block behind the aortic valve, making it very hard for blood to pump into the body. At this point I was told that it would be a miracle if my baby made it to 28 weeks.

28 weeks came along, and I could still feel her moving. At the doctor's appointment he was shocked. He informed me of all the risks still ahead, and told me that I should be aware of her movement all the time. If she stopped moving at any time, I needed to come immediately. He was positive she would not make it to birth.

At 32 weeks, I went back, and he set the C-section to be done at 39 weeks. I was informed that she would more than likely be born blue and I would not be allowed to see her; she would leave me and go directly into the NICU where she would receive a ventilator and an external pacemaker until the doctors had a chance to do an echo on her. This of course was if she would make it through delivery at all.

Madison was born September 24th, 2008 at 12:23 pm. She was 6 lbs., 13ozs. and 20 1/2 inches long. She was not blue, did not need an immediate ventilator or a pacemaker. She lived her first two days without the two.

During a visit with Madison on the 26th, the doctors came in and informed us that her oxygen levels were dropping and she needed a ventilator. As soon as we were able to go back in, my husband and I stood back and watched as our daughter went into cardiac arrest and the doctors performed CPR.

Earlier that day, the surgeon, Dr. Bichell, an amazing surgeon, came to talk to us and informed us that the surgery he would be performing would not be a simple task to say the least. He informed us that all the diagnoses that she had were common, however none of them have ever been reported together. He explained to us that he was going to do a surgery that he had never performed before, and that he couldn't find any reports on any doctors ever performing anything of the sort.

After going into cardiac arrest and being revived, Madison was rushed to the OR for open heart surgery. We were told it would be around five hours before she would be out. That was around 12:30 pm.

At 7 pm, we got a call letting us know that she was doing well and that she would be out of surgery soon. At 8 pm we received another call; she was out of surgery, however she would have to be put on a machine called ECMO.

For those of you who don't know, ECMO is much like the heart and lung bypass machine that they use during open heart surgeries. This machine would work alongside the heart, doing 90 percent of the work for her. Through one tube, the blood would be taken out of her body and run through a machine and then inserted back into the body through another tube. They informed us that she could only stay on this machine for a very short period of time, and that it was imperative that she get off of it as soon as she was able.

Six days later, Madison was taken off the ECMO. The doctors came out, told us she had been off for almost an hour and was doing great. We were so relieved. We were left to wait for them to finish in the room before we could go in. 10 minutes went by and we got a call to come in. We walked in to find about 10 doctors in the room surrounding her and watching her monitor very closely. They explained to us that Madison's blood pressure was borderline and they were contemplating putting her back on ECMO. They feared she would not make it through the night if they left her off of it.

She was on ECMO for another four days, this time when they took her off the machine, she stayed off! Again we were relieved. We had been told that any longer and she may start to lose function of her other organs.

As relieved as we were, it was only two days before they were back, this time with a dialysis machine. They were using dialysis to pull off some of the fluids she had built up. They also added a few drainage tubes to help relieve the fluids. They were hopeful that the kidneys, which had stopped working due to the ECMO machine, would come back on their own.

Over the next couple of days they did several procedures in her room to clean out around the heart and relieve some of the pressure off of it. They had her blood pressure medications turned up as high as her body could handle. They had taken her off morphine and onto the strongest they could possibly give a baby, and the most that she could have. They did another echo on her heart and found that the right side had pretty much stopped functioning altogether.

A team of doctors; a cardiologist, a kidney doctor, a nurse, a social worker, and one other doctor came in to speak with us and talk about Madison. They informed us that Madison's kidneys were completely gone. At this point there was no hope for a return for them. She also, at this point was diagnosed with liver failure, and as I mentioned before, the right side of her heart was not functioning. It was not a matter of should we disconnect, it was more a matter of when to disconnect.

We decided on Tuesday, the 21st of October. That Sunday, during a visit with Madison, the doctors came in and informed us they did not believe she would make it until Tuesday. My husband and I stayed that night with her and all our family came in. We were all able to hold her as long as we wanted. Once disconnected, Madison only lived 20 minutes. Madison Abigail passed away October 20, 2008 at 2:50 pm in my arms.

The hardest thing for me was/is:

My husband was deployed during my pregnancy and I already had another baby at home. She was so sick, but I felt as a parent and a believer in God, that there was a reason I was given the situation and that my child deserved a chance at life. Other people didn't really understand. The doctors, though hopeful, had to keep the reality of the situation in my mind. Having them tell you that your baby wouldn't make it to certain dates *is* the hardest thing ever as a mom.

After she was born, it was almost unbearable to watch such an innocent and precious baby suffering. I knew she wasn't hurting, but how could a baby with all those tubes and machines hooked up to her, not be suffering? Also, the roller coaster of her progress; she would be doing better one day, and then not so great the next. The question of, when is enough, enough? How do you answer that? How do you *pick* the day your child will pass on? I wanted so badly for our families to see her and have the chance to hold her before she passed. At that time, it seemed right for our family, but I know now she was suffering.

Helpful things that family and friends did that I will forever be grateful for:

They helped with my older daughter. I never had to look for babysitters for appointments. And when I was in that room holding my baby girl, a family member took my older daughter so that I could focus on what was going on.

Things that have helped me cope and deal with the heartache:

I turned to God. My little girl was a miracle. God blessed me with her. I don't know why he chose us, and I will never know. I think often of what her life would be like now. It only takes a second to realize she would have been miserable. Madison was one year younger than her sister. She would have always been left at home because of the precautions needed to take care of her. Her development would have been *very* delayed. She now is in heaven; no tubes, no bruises, no pacemaker. She is *perfect* in every way possible.

What I have learned from this:

Show your children how much you love them. Remember that every minute counts. My biggest regret is that I didn't hold her just a little bit longer. I now give my child a hug and kiss every morning. And I thank God everyday for the blessings in my life, including my guardian angel.

How I keep my infant's memory alive:

We talk about her all the time. Madison was cremated. Her ashes were placed into a teddy bear. We chose that because we are still a young, military couple. We still have a long time in the military and many moves to make. I don't have to visit a grave site to visit my baby girl. She's with us always. Her bear sits in our family room on display. I also share her story proudly with anyone who asks. I feel that sharing her story is a good way to help other parents realize that what they have is precious.

Additional words to help others dealing with the loss of their infant:

Remember that things always happen for reasons. God does not punish us. He rewards us with the opportunity to share our love with these amazing children. There are no tests of your strength, rather a show in which you get to know your strength and yourself. God has a plan for each and every one of us. Allow your child to become your inspiration and motivation in whatever you do.

~ Danielle Paqueo ~

**The LORD will give strength unto his people;
the LORD will bless his people with peace.**

Psalms 29:11

16

Easton Wayne-Lee Hepburn

November 2, 2006 – February 20, 2007

My Story:

Easton was born at 27 weeks weighting 2 lbs., 8 ozs. and was so sweet. He lived in the NICU for two months as he overcame many challenges such as a blown lung. He also had a grade-4 brain bleed and would have to have a shunt put in. I watched this little miracle grow and thrive into a wonderful little angel right before my eyes. He was such a little "trooper" as my sister would call him. He came home on Jan 3rd, 2007 weighting 5lbs., 12 ozs. He grew so much over the last two months that I just knew he was going to grow up like his brothers. Then my world turned upside down again. On February 19th, Easton went in for a routine check-up just like any month. This time they were concerned about his temperature being too low. They told us that with a low temp in preemies, it could show a sign of infection so we were moved to the children's hospital downtown. When we arrived, he was alert and crying because he knew it was time to eat. At 6 pm on February 19th, the doctor finally came in and said that he wanted to run some blood work; that his shunt might have an infection in it. When he had it put in they told us that this could happen. So the nurses came in to take blood from him. After about two hours, the doctor came in to tell us that Easton was in acute kidney failure and needed to be put on CVVH as soon as we could get him upstairs to ICU. I was so upset with this news I didn't understand how. At 11pm on February 19th, my little man was moved to ICU; never did I think that this would be the last time I saw him crying and looking into my eyes. They told us to wait in the waiting room until they got him on the CVVH machine. They told us it would take about an hour, so we waited. After three hours of waiting the doctor came out and told us that they were having a hard time putting him on the machine and it would be a little longer. After about 45 more minutes of waiting the doctor came out and told us that Easton's heart had stopped and he was losing blood and they didn't know why. So I signed a blood transfusion form. Then the doctor came back about 15 minutes later and told us that Easton's heart was beating again. At 4 am on February 20th, the nurses came to get my husband and I and I knew by the look on their face what was happening. My little Easton was going to grow his wings in to heaven. And he did. At 4:36 am little Easton grew his wings into heaven. They moved us to a room where we could spend time with him and family came to be with us. I held on to him for 10 hours, not wanting to let go. The doctor came in as we were getting ready to leave and asked us if we wanted an autopsy done to find the cause of the kidney failure and we decided that we wanted to know. After six weeks of waiting, the results came in and shocked us all. Easton was born with only one, working kidney and we never knew it so his one working kidney was not strong enough to keep up with his body. Then we also found out that he bled to death by a hole in his heart from the centerline that the doctor tried to put in. It killed me knowing, that because tests were not run; my little baby was in heaven. I love and miss you Easton; Mommy loves you.

The hardest thing for me is:

Still today, that I do not have that relationship with Easton like I do with Logan, Cason and Weston. Holidays are also very hard for me because I always tell myself I should he buying four Easter baskets, not three. I am still coping with Easton angel day, one day at a time.

Helpful thing that family and friends did that I will forever be grateful for:

The night of Easton's visitation, a friend of mine that I was very close to in school but haven't talked much since, came and she gave me a Beanie Baby cat because I loved cats and Easton would watch our cat all the time, just following her everywhere while he was swinging. She brought me two of them; one for me and one for Easton to sleep with in heaven. She said if I ever needed a hug I could hug this cat and would know that he was hugging his cat at the same time and it would be like hugging him. I love her for that and to this day when I am having a bad day I will sit, hold and hug this cat knowing he is hugging his cat at the same time.

Things that have helped me cope:

Is that my family is always there. I could not make it without them. They are there if I need to talk, cry, scream or whatever I need; they are there. My boys Logan, Cason and Weston are my rock. I look at them every day and thanks God for giving me three, beautiful healthy boys and a wonderful angel in heaven looking down on us every day. I have talked to some people that have lost a child and it has helped knowing that there are other mothers out there that know how I feel about losing a child.

What I have learned from this:

I know that children are priceless and to cherish every minute that you have with them. I believe that mothers who have lost children are the lucky ones. We have an angel watching over us daily and not everyone can say that about a child. Easton will always be my angel watching over me and I see him in Logan, Cason and Weston.

How I keep Easton's memory alive:

On his birthday we have a balloon release and then we all go out to eat and have a birthday cake. For Christmas, we buy for a boy that is Easton's age and born in November. So at Christmas I buy for a little boy who would not have if we didn't buy for him. We do this in Easton's memory: every two months we change out the flowers at the cemetery. We had a memory tree planted and dedicated in Easton's memory at our local city park with a plaque. We have a memory lamp that is made with the flowers from his funeral and we burn it all the time; we never turn it off. On February 20th, we spend it with the boys doing something that they want to do so that we are just not thinking about what the day; it is loving our children. Easton is remembered every day of the year. His memory will always be remembered and never forgotten. These traditions will never change.

Additional words to help others dealing with the loss of their infant:

The one thing that I can say to other mothers who have lost a child: live one day at a time. Don't think about what you are going to do next week or what about Easter or Christmas. Just remember him or her every day and say I love you and will never forget you. This does not take the pain away, but it lets you know that no matter what we love our angel babies. Losing a child is something that no one should ever have to go through, but some of our children are taken away to heaven to play in the garden and to watch over us. I played Kenny Chesney's song *Who you'd be today* at the funeral and like the song says "the only thing that gives me hope is that I know I'll see you again someday." To all the mothers who have lost a child: When I light a candle for Easton I will think about all of Easton's angel friends looking down on us every day; in memory of Easton Wayne Lee Hepburn. Mommy loves you and misses you every day. I am sending you kisses and hugs to Heaven.

~ Casey Hepburn ~

Footprints

"These are my footprints,
so perfect and so small.
These tiny footprints
never touched the ground at all.
Not one tiny footprint,
for now I have wings.
These tiny footprints were meant
for other things.
You will hear my tiny footprints,
in the patter of the rain.
Gentle drops like angel's tears,
of joy and not from pain.
You will see my tiny footprints,
in each butterflies' lazy dance.
I'll let you know I'm with you,
if you just give me the chance.
You will see my tiny footprints,
in the rustle of the leaves.
I will whisper names into the wind,
and call each one that grieves.
Most of all, these tiny footprints,
are found on Mommy and Daddy's hearts.
'Cause even though I'm gone now,
We'll never truly part."

Author Unknown

17

Shawna Lynn Morris

December 31, 1987 - February 21, 1988

My Story:

Shawna arrived on Thursday, December 31, 1987. I was thrilled. I had two boys already and I finally got my little girl. She was a beautiful baby and perfect in every way. Shawna was such an easy baby; never fussy, sleeping almost completely through the night (at just a little over one month); happy and content all the time. Her older brothers, Michael and Brent, who were three and two at the time, doted on her. I couldn't have been happier.

On Sunday morning, February 21, 1988, I woke a little later than usual. Shawna had not woken me up at all during the night, which wasn't really out of the ordinary, and I walked over to her bassinet to check on her (her bassinet was in my room). What I found was every parent's worst nightmare. Shawna had rolled up against the side of her bassinet and it looked like the mattress had somehow been pulled slightly out from under her. She wasn't breathing and it was fairly obvious that she had been like that for a while. I called 911 and she was rushed to the hospital. The doctors worked on her for some time, but eventually told me what I already knew in my heart, that she had died.

My first thought, based on her position in the bassinet, was that she had suffocated. I couldn't fathom how the mattress moved the way it had. As Colorado has a law that requires autopsies on all children, the hospital had the county coroner come in to talk to me. He explained to me, based on his initial observations, that he thought Shawna had died of Sudden Infant Death Syndrome (SIDS) but he would know more after he completed the autopsy. The results came back that is was SIDS. Basically, what they found was a healthy baby with absolutely no indication as to what might have gone wrong, which is the determining factor in SIDS deaths.

The week that followed passed in a blur. Having to make funeral arrangements for your child is something parents should never have to go through. I kept thinking that this was all a nightmare and that eventually I would wake up and everything would be fine; that Shawna would still be with me, if only that would have been the case.

The hardest thing about losing an infant, (Shawna only lived for 7 1/2 weeks) is not getting to see all the firsts; the first tooth, the first steps, the first words, starting kindergarten and the list just goes on and on. In the beginning I had real trouble being around other babies. Seeing other babies was a very real and painful reminder that I no longer had Shawna with me. After a few years I was able to see other babies and even take joy in being around them. There are still moments that seeing someone else's baby brings everything back, but nothing like the horrible feeling I used to get in the first few years. Still, the hardest day of the year for me is the anniversary of Shawna's death. Her birthday is always bittersweet, but the death date is still unbelievably hard, even after all the years that have passed.

I was lucky in the fact that I had my two young sons at home. I had to stay focused and strong to take care of them. I think they helped me keep my sanity! We also became involved in a support group for SIDS parents. Being around people that are dealing with the same emotional issues that you are is incredibly helpful. You don't feel so alone and isolated. The emotional support is so important in helping you cope with such a tragic event. I met parents that had been dealing with their loss for numerous years and it was comforting to realize that you can get through it. The hurt never completely goes away, but being around other people that have experienced the same thing makes you realize that you can begin the healing process.

One of the hardest things for me was family, friends and co-workers who became uncomfortable around me after Shawna died. There were some people who would quickly try to change the subject whenever I mentioned Shawna's name. I can't even begin to completely explain the pain that caused. It made me feel as though some people could care less that she ever existed. Others, though, genuinely encouraged me to talk about her and were always there to listen, to comfort or to just lend a shoulder to cry on. Because of some people, too many people's discomfort in hearing about an infant death, I initially had a very hard time in answering the simple question "How many children do you have?" That question always seems to lead to "How old are they?" and "How many boys or girls do you have?" I used to answer three; two sons and a daughter in heaven. Unfortunately, the obvious discomfort and sometimes embarrassment some people reacted with caused me to stop mentioning Shawna when I would get those questions. It took me several years to realize that including Shawna in the how many children questions was more important than worrying about the feelings of those that asked.

On what would have been Shawna's first birthday, we took balloons out to her grave and let them go. Michael and Brent watched them until they could no longer be seen. At that time they concluded that Shawna got her balloons. That became a yearly custom on her birthday, sending balloons to Shawna. Eight years after Shawna's death I finally worked up the courage to have another baby. My second daughter, Kayla, was born in 1996. Even though she never met her older sister she has been sending balloons to Shawna ever since she was a very small girl. The first time it happened she was about four and she accidentally let go of the string on her balloon and started to cry. But she stopped crying just as quickly and said that Shawna could have her balloon now. Ever since that time she would give Shawna every balloon she ever got. Shawna is buried in Colorado and we have been in California since 1999. I don't get a chance to make it to the cemetery very often but, no matter where we are, we still send Shawna her balloons on her birthday, and always wait until she receives them.

Simple little things, like the balloons, keep Shawna's memory alive. Sharing her short life by talking about her is also a very important manner of remembering her. Talking to and trying to help others who have had a baby die, as others did for me, helps me as well. I can never have Shawna back, but I will always have the sweet memories of her. Nothing can ever take that away.

~ Kimberly Soto ~

Therefore being justified by faith,
we have peace with God through our Lord Jesus Christ:
By whom also we have access by faith into this grace
wherein we stand, and rejoice in hope of the glory of God.
And not only so, but we glory in tribulations also:
knowing that tribulation worketh
patience;
And patience, experience; and experience, hope:
And hope maketh not ashamed; because the love
of God is shed abroad in our hearts by the
Holy Ghost which is given unto us.

Romans 5:1-5

18

Gilberto Chavarria III (Pito)

July 29, 2001 - February 5, 2002

My story:

My baby boy was born on July 29th, 2001 at 7:30 am. He was beautiful! He had a little bit of a rough start though. During my pregnancy, we found out that he had a condition called gastroschisis, a birth defect that caused his intestines to stick out of his body through a defect on one side of his umbilical cord. As soon as he was delivered, he was taken into surgery and it was repaired with absolutely no problems. We brought him home three weeks later.

On February 5th, we started our day as we normally did. We woke up at 6 am like we had every morning to get the kids to the babysitters and head off to work. Once I got my baby boy ready, I put him in his car seat on the couch so that I could get started with his sister. As I was going back and forth through the house getting their things ready, he caught my attention. I looked at him and smiled and I told him how beautiful he was. In return, he gave me the most beautiful smile! That moment has for ever been etched in my mind. We got the kids to the babysitter and got them settled, before we left I told him that I loved him...little did I realize that those would be my last words to him.

About an hour after I got to work, my husband stormed in with a look of panic on his face and told me we had to go, we ran to our truck and took off. On the way I ask him what was going on...all he said was "Mijo isn't breathing!" I think I went into some kind of shock because I had no emotion...it just wouldn't register in my brain. When we finally got to the babysitter's house, I jumped out and ran inside. My two-year-old daughter was sitting on the couch crying. There were people everywhere and I couldn't find my son. Finally they took me to the room where he had been taking a nap. The paramedics wouldn't let me in...all I could see was a paramedic performing CPR on him...he was blocking my view of my baby's face...all I could see was his naked little body in his pamper. After a few minutes they brought him out of the room and took him to the ambulance. I rode in the ambulance with him and my husband drove in the truck. On the way to the hospital, one of the paramedics asked me how long he had had a cold. When I told him that he didn't have a cold, the look on his face changed...I think he knew. When we got there, they rushed him in and took me in the opposite direction into the waiting room. It seemed like I was in there forever. Finally they came for me, but only to take me into another room...an office. Again I waited, and waited. My husband, meanwhile, still wasn't at the hospital. After a while, someone came in and asked me if I wanted to have my son baptized *just in case*, I said yes and again...waited. Finally a nurse came and led me to where they were still working on him. As I walked in, I noticed the chaplain was already there baptizing him while they were still doing CPR...I kept telling him that mommy was there with him and that I needed him to wake up. That's when the doctor stopped, turned to me and said those God-awful words... "I'm sorry." I wanted to hit him *so* bad! I screamed at the top of my lungs, "No, Jesus, No!" I fell to my knees; I was so weak. I just kept calling for my Jesus and yelling. They took me to an examining room to calm down and wait some more. After a while, they brought my baby in to me to hold one more time...I don't know if this makes any sense, but when the nurse handed him to me...he was empty. I knew he wasn't in there. I know it sounds crazy, but I don't know. While I was holding him, I cut a lock of his hair and they took a couple of pictures of me holding him. My husband finally arrived after going to the wrong hospital and walked in to see me holding our baby's lifeless body; it was the worst day of our lives. I was so numb. I had no feeling. I couldn't cry. I couldn't feel anything; anything after that I really don't remember. I know our daughter was traumatized. For two nights, she woke up screaming in terror. After that she started sucking on her finger. That went on until she was about five-years-old. She's 11 now and still cries for her brother. I know she really doesn't remember much about him, but I think it just hurts her to know that he's gone.

The hardest thing for me:

Afterwards....the next year-and-a-half was the hardest. I didn't have anyone to talk to and no one knew what I was going through. People kept pretty much telling me to get over it; he was gone and there was nothing that I could do. I also had a lot of guilt. I didn't like to let him sleep on his stomach because of the gastroschisis. The baby sitter had also asked me if there was a particular way that I didn't want him to sleep and I said no....so I felt it was my fault for not telling her not to put him on his tummy.

What I learned from this:

There is a God and my baby is with him! Before this, I would wonder if there was a God. Through this whole experience I gained a relationship with Him and without Him I would *never* have gotten through this. And it wasn't God who did this. It took me a long time to learn that *I didn't do anything wrong*. Once I got tired of crying, I realized that I had to stop holding on to him and I had to let God have him, *That's* when it started getting easier...I know my baby is waiting for me; that's what keeps me going. Don't get me wrong, I still cry, I miss him so much; his smiling face, his laugh, his scar on his tummy from his surgery, the mole on his leg...I could go on forever, but I know I will see him again!

How I keep my infant's memory alive:

I talk about him all the time. Since then I've had two more daughters and they both know about their brother. We also have a *huge* airbrushed painting of him.

Additional words to help others dealing with the loss of their infant:

Psalm 55:12, Cast your cares on the Lord and He will sustain you; Jeremiah 29:11, *For I know the plans I have for you, plans for good and not for evil, to give you a future and a hope*; Isaiah 41:10, *Fear not, for I am with you; be not dismayed, for I am your God. I will strengthen you; I will uphold you with My righteous hand.*

I am comforted when I think that my Creator knows exactly what I'm going through, He did it when He watched His Son die on the cross for us. Always know that you are not alone; if you have no one to talk to, there is *One* who will listen and who knows exactly what you're going through. I pray that God gives you His peace that surpasses all understanding and that He wrap His arm around you and bring you comfort. And please know that *it's OK to cry*!

~ Genie Chavarria ~

Precious Little One,

We had you in our lives such a very short time,
but we'll hold you in our hearts forever.
It seemed like only a fleeting moment,
but it was long enough to see you,
touch you, hold you, love you.
It was long enough to know that
your life was indeed a gift -
no matter how brief,
no matter how fragile,
Your life was indeed a gift,
and we'll hold you in our hearts forever.

Author Unknown

19

Justin Glover

November 22, 2002 - February 6, 2003

My Story:

My son passed away of SIDS. I was at work the night it happened; my husband was the one at home. There are some days I wished I would have been at home with my family instead of at work taking care of other people's loved ones. But then again I am not so sure I could have made that call, or done CPR on my son. My husband handled that situation better than I ever could have. I still miss my son, but I have an older son that I have diverted my attention to.

Helpful things that family and friends did that I will forever be grateful for:

My family showing up at my house and trying to help out was the best they could in our time of need, and is something I will be forever grateful for. Having a sister and a mother-in-law, who had gone through something similar, helped out even more.

Things that have helped me cope and deal with the heartache:

For a while we attended a group therapy session, but that did not help nearly as much as having a preacher to talk to and a mother-in-law and sister to be there for us to give us support when needed.

What I have learned from this:

My family and I have learned that nothing in this life is guaranteed and that we have a home waiting in heaven where we are guaranteed to see our son again.

How I keep my infant's memory alive:

We keep his memory alive by going to his grave on his birthday and each one of us let a balloon go in honor of him after we tell what we are thankful for. I am just thankful to have gotten to spend time with my son while he was on this earth. Every holiday we try to go to his grave and clean it up real well and decorate it with stuff for that day.

Additional words to help others dealing with the loss of their infant:

There is nothing we can do to change what happened yesterday, but we can live for today and enjoy the rest of our life on this earth while looking forward to being reunited with loved ones in heaven. I realize there is nothing I can do to bring back my youngest son, but out of that whole terrible event I learned not to take my loved ones for granted and to enjoy every minute I have with them because we are not guaranteed one more day with them. We just have today and I try to make the best of each day cherishing every moment I am blessed to spend yet another day with friends and loved ones.

~ Cheril Glover ~

They that sow in tears shall reap in joy.

Psalms 126:5

20

Ashleigh Krystin Noyes

November 30, 1993 - February 2, 1994

My Story:

My daughter Ashleigh was born the last day of November in 1993. I had begged the doctor to do a C-section on my wife at the time, Karen so that the baby would be born on my father-in-law's birthday. Looking back there was a reason she was not. Karen was in labor for almost 24 hours before our first daughter came into our world. Ashleigh's birth was no picnic. Ashleigh went into fetal stress. This was a scary moment, and not my only experience. A year later I went through it with our second daughter. Upon Ashleigh's arrival, it seemed like time stopped for a moment. I remember the nurse asking me to carry Ashleigh down to the nursery to be checked over. I took my daughter into my arms and started my way down the hall. During this short walk, it seemed like forever. I saw Ashleigh's whole life in front of me. I saw my daughter take her first step. I watched Ashleigh board the school bus for her first day of school. I took a few more steps down that hall way, and I visualized her graduating high school, then more years past. Before I entered the nursery to lay her down on the scales, the last thing I saw was the two of us walking down a church aisle; my baby was getting married. I left my first born in the nursery to be taken care. I walked back to my Karen's room and was thinking that is the strangest thing in life I have ever experienced. Two months later, that dream or visualization was destroyed; my Ashleigh was called home elsewhere and taken away from us.

In the short two months that my daughter was here, it seemed like a much longer time. Everyone would look at Ashleigh and say how beautiful she was, but most everyone would say, she's an angel and looks older than she is. Ashleigh's only Christmas was special; this was really the only holiday that she celebrated.

I remember February 2nd, 1994 like it was yesterday. I remember getting up out of bed and saying goodbye to Ashleigh before she went to daycare. This particular morning, I remember kissing her good bye and talking to her. Right before I was getting ready to go back to bed, Ashleigh gave me the strangest look. I looked at her and it scared me. I told her to stop looking at me that way. I didn't know she was trying to tell me something. That afternoon I was getting myself ready to head to work and the telephone rang. I answered it and Karen told me I was needed at the emergency room immediately, my daughter was there. Karen didn't have many details, therefore, didn't tell me all that much, but said to come quickly. I got in my jeep and headed down to the hospital. On my drive there something told me that things were not right. I knew that I would never be able to spend any more time with my first born.

I entered the emergency room and was escorted to a room where Karen and my mother-in-law were waiting. I was told it didn't look good. My mother-in-law told me what she encountered upon picking her up at child care. I remember when doctor-poor-bedside-manner came in and said, "she's dead." I collapsed; I was on the floor crying and screaming. The day before, I had attended, who I called my grandmother's, funeral. I just couldn't take another loss, not that quickly and not my own daughter. I finally came out of it. Karen did think that they might have to admit me; she was that worried. That evening and several days later we were surrounded by love ones. A winter death is the hardest; you go through the funeral, and then in the spring you have to go through it all over again with the burial. We buried my daughter and her great God-mother the same day. It was another hard day to encounter. I was walking my daughter down an aisle; it was an aisle to her grave, not down the church aisle like I had visualized the morning she was born. After her burial for many days, weeks, and months, I would find myself standing at her grave talking to her, and asking God why.

A year later I was blessed with another daughter, Krystin, Ashleigh's middle name.

It's been 17 years now and I still remember everything like it was yesterday. I hope that my heartache and pain can help someone else and let them know that they are not alone and have people that have experienced heartache and pain also.

The hardest thing for me was/is:

The hardest thing for me was the last morning Ashleigh was here with us. The look that she gave me was a look that I never want to see again or in anyone else. Looking back, Ashleigh was trying to say goodbye to me in the only manner she could, that was in her eyes and facial expression. The other hardest part was walking her down the aisle to her grave, it just wasn't right; she was not with us long enough. My life dreams for her were shattered.

Helpful things that family and friends did that I will forever be grateful for:

During the terrible time that was brought upon us, our family and close friends were there throughout the whole ordeal. Our parents were there being as strong and supportive after all they were dealing with the same loss as we were. It was just as hard for them as it was for us. Not only did they lose a grandchild, they had to see us go through the pain of losing our daughter. We had friends coming from everywhere and we had tons of food being dropped off. There were tons of cards coming in. The funeral home went above and beyond. Our family, friends and people we did not even know were sending money to the SIDS foundation in the memory of Ashleigh. Karen and I decided not to return to our home for a while; we just were not ready to go back to our home now that it was going to be just the two of us. When we did return home, my dad, a co-worker of his and our two best friends, had gone into our home and removed all items that were associated with Ashleigh. They put all the items in her room and shut the door. In time when we were ready we could enter the room and face reality.

Things that have helped me cope and deal with the heartache:

Karen and I were contacted by people of the SIDS group in Portland. It was difficult at first to attend, but after we had been to a few monthly meetings we were opening up and sharing our loss with others. Not only were we sharing our loss, but we were also helping couples that had recently lost a child as well. We attended every Christmas remembrance that they had; sad part that this came to an end.

When our daughter Krystin was born, we started a tradition. Her first birthday, which was a year and ten days apart, we let balloons off to heaven for Ashleigh to celebrate her birthday as well. Krystin and I did this for many years to come. We let them go on November 30th and February 2nd. Several years later I had met a sweet older woman who was suffering Alzheimer's. I spent many of my days with her and her family. I grew very close to her and her loved ones. On February 2nd, she was losing her battle for life. I remember going to her before I went to work that night and spoke to her letting her know that I asked my angel to help her come into the light with her other love ones; she too passed away on February 2nd. I also passed on the balloon tradition to that family. Krystin has grown older, and we are not always available on Ashleigh's dates so the balloons have ended. I have now started a new tradition of toasting to her memory with a glass of wine.

What I have learned from this:

We never know what life is going to set before us. Life as we know it, can be very short. The hardest part is that we will never know why our young loved ones are taken from us. I have also learned not to judge others; we all go through difficult times differently. Some of us take it harder than others. Some of us go on with life in different ways after the loss of our loved one.

How I keep my infant's memory alive:

I keep Ashleigh's memory alive each and every day. I have her pictures up so that I can see them. Ashleigh's memories are embedded in my brain and I hope nothing happens so that I will never lose them. I know that she is my guardian angel and she has helped me several times in close calls. I feel her presence mostly when I am in a vehicle now. I also see a part of her in Krystin. Several months after Krystin was born it seemed like Ashleigh had come back to us. Though I knew that was not true; they were very much alike. I also keep her memory alive when I am talking to people who ask how many children I have. I always answer two. I have one here on earth and one in heaven above.

I still remember the two dates, November 30th and February 2nd; from balloons to now toasting her with a glass of wine.

Additional words to help others dealing with the loss of their infant:

To those who have lost a love one, the only thing I can tell you, is to do what you think is best for you. Don't let people tell you how you feel or let them push you into getting back to life. You know what you need to do. It seems to us that life has stopped because we have lost our loved one, and as much as we want that to be true, life continues to keep going. It will not stop for us. It seems unfair and we don't understand, but for some reason it's a lesson in life for us. We need to be happy that we were granted what time we had with our loved ones and be blessed with that.

~Barry Noyes~

“What we have once enjoyed we can never lose. All that we love deeply becomes a part of us.”

Helen Keller

21

Shannen Anne Milliken,

August 18, 1996 – December 9, 2003

Niall Craig Milliken,

March 31, 1999 – December 9, 2003

Adon Milliken & Ethan Milliken

July 26, 2007 - Stillborn

My Story:

How do I even begin to describe in words what has happened in my life? I am almost too scared to tell anyone as it sounds like it is almost out of a science fiction movie. My husband, John and I were married in December, 1994. I fell pregnant and was ecstatic. I prayed for my child from the time of conception. I used to get the bible and read bible verses to her all the time. Somehow from the beginning of my pregnancy I knew it was a girl – a precious girl. She was born on the 18th of August 1996, a perfectly healthy little baby girl with the most gorgeous red hair and blue eyes. She was born with a cleft lip. Dr Davey, the plastic surgeon, did about three operations on Shannen's lip starting when she was one-year-old - he did a lovely job and at the age of seven you could not see that Shannen had had a cleft lip. Shannen was such a joy to the whole family. She had the most amazing nature - often mother's would tell me that she is an angel on earth. I have to say I would get upset with this because I knew that those children were always taken to heaven early, so I tried to brush off those comments. I never had a day of trouble with Shannen. God had given me a wonderful child; an angel on earth.

I gave up work for her and started to look after her full time at home. What a joy. I look back at those years and just smile. God certainly blessed me. All the time in the back of my mind, I was reminding myself that God has given me this child; that this child does not belong to me. I used to tell this to Shannen often, which would give her great excitement.

I was then blessed with another most amazing gift - a son. My beautiful son was born on the March 31, 1999. What a funny, curious, naughty little boy with blond hair and big blue eyes. Anyone who came into contact with this child would never forget him. He had this knack of being remembered - he was usually screaming or climbing something.

So here I am a housewife, a mother and loving every minute of my children. I remember driving in my car one day and saying to God, "I have found my calling; it is to be a mother." Oh I just loved being a mother. However, every day I would tell my children about Jesus, we would pray and I would then tell them that they did not belong to me, they belonged to God and God had chosen me to bring them up on this earth. I look back now and know that I knew something was going to happen - there was a *check* in my spirit.

John, my husband was the perfect father and husband. He provided financially for us, enough so that I could stay at home and look after the children. Both the children were the "apple of his eye" and he always made time for them and always played with them. We made so many good memories. Thank God for the memories. I could carry on and on with the funny memories. I thank God, He taught us to make memories and not money.

Accident - The most horrific, traumatic, worst day of my life!

The great sadness. The day our lives changed; the day you never want to happen. The day no parent wants to go through. December, 9th, 2003. We are in Durban on holiday. We have just been out shopping for Christmas presents and getting very excited about Christmas. On the way back to our house on the south coast, just outside of Port Edward, Niall had an epileptic seizure and I had to get into the back seat and resuscitate him. My husband turns the car around and we take him to the Margate hospital where tests are done on him. I am in a total state of shock and shaking from head to toe. The doctor releases us, but wants to see Niall in two days time - the day that never comes.

The whole family gets back into the car – that is John, me, Shannen, Niall and my mother-in-law Ann. I am in the back seat with Niall and Shannen. Ann decides she wants to swap seats with me, but I do not want to; I want to sit in the back. She absolutely insists and just gets into the back seat, forcing me to the front seat. A couple of minutes down the road, I turn to my babies and I touch both of them and I say, for the last time "I love you guys so much, you know that, don't you?" They both acknowledge that they know that their mother loves them and they almost roll their eyes because I am always saying that!

Then the crunch of metal. I go unconscious, I wake up; there is silence in my car. No crying, no talking. I am sorry I cannot describe to the reader the scene before my eyes, it is too traumatic for me to repeat. Devastation. Niall died on impact (five minutes before I was sitting in that seat), Shannen died a couple of minutes later and Ann died about ten minutes later. All I can remember is running up and down the road praying and shouting, "No Jesus, don't do this, no Jesus, no Jesus." Unfortunately, there was no miracle; there was no bolt of lightning. Both my children went to heaven at the scene of the accident along with their Gran. It was comforting for me to know that their Gran went with them. I remember holding my dead children in my arms and just thinking, *How am I going to live without them; how am I going to carry on, this is a dream.* The last I saw of Niall was with blood coming out of his mouth and ears. The last I saw of

Shannen was the paramedics covering her up with a blanket and her foot sticking out the bottom. As I write these words I am crying and there are still things I cannot talk about. I walked away from the scene of the accident when I knew both my children were dead - I remember turning around, in a dream state and looking at the carnage. Blood all over the road, blood all over me - I distinctly remember the presence of God standing next to me. God said to me in an audible voice, "It is finished, they are with me now." Turning around I walked up the hill to a garage and sat there in total shock. My brain stopped working, I went dizzy and everything is a blur. I remember the paramedics coming to my husband and me much later, after they had tried to save my children and Ann. As I was covered from head-to-toe in blood they had to check where the blood was coming from - in a very calm voice, I said "it's not my blood; it's my babies' blood." The paramedics then took us to the ambulance, but before they could put us in an ambulance they had to take the dead bodies out first. Oh what a trauma to know that your children are now referred to as "dead bodies."

Once in the ambulance I went into shock and had to be sedated and put on oxygen. I also had a neck brace on and they thought I had broken my leg. My husband, John only discovered then that he had a piercing pain in his chest which turned out to be a broken rib. On arrival at the Margate Hospital, my husband and I were both put into the same room - my husband then went into shock and I thought he was dying. I went into a total panic thinking that now my whole family was going to die. John was stabilized and we were left in a private room where we were sedated. The Police followed us to the hospital and advised me that Shannen, Niall and Ann's bodies had been taken to the mortuary. The bodies could only be released after having been identified by a family member. The thought of my babies being in a mortuary traumatized me even more, how could they be in a mortuary; alone.

My mother and father arrived the next day at ten in the morning, followed closely by John's sister, Tara and brother, Bruce. The whole family was just in total shock. I just have to tell you what Karen, my sister, saw. She ran out the house on receiving the phone call - she looked up to the heavens and said to God, "*Why*?" As she looked up, Karen saw three figures standing, holding hands. This was confirmation to her that Shannen, Niall and Ann had gone to heaven and were safe.

So we go on holiday and I come home with three boxes of ashes... it was devastating.

During all this time, you are still in a state of shock and you expect your child to come around the corner at any time, so you are in denial and still in shock and nothing seemed to be sinking in.

The South African police did a complete forensic report on the accident and it was proved, beyond doubt, that the other driver was at fault and John could have no way avoided the collision. This was a huge relief for my husband as he felt he had killed his own children and failed to protect them. The police were amazing and went above and beyond their call of duty. What I remember the most is the compassion they showed us and the support they gave us during the first days of our grief.

People from John's company were so great at this time. Colin Armstrong, Alan Stevenson and the Stancom pilot went out of their way to organize a plane for us to fly home. The pilot took time off from his holiday and came and flew us all home. This was a great help as we could not bear to be in a cramped plane with people we did not know carrying three little boxes of ashes.

On arrival at home, Harare, we were just surrounded by friends and family. All the time in my head I'm thinking, *no, I can do this, this is ok, I can manage this.* Little did I know that a year later it would sink in. As our trauma was so great my brain could not take in all the information and so it temporarily closed down for about a year – so things are a blur, but I will try and remember events as they happened.

Tuesday, December 19th was the day of the funeral that we held at Highlands Presbyterian Church. I remember looking in the sky that day and it was about to rain. I said to God, "Please of all the days do not let it rain today." I have to tell you that it did not rain. I remember arriving at the church in a daze and thinking all these people are here for US, for my family, for my children. I was amazed. The church was full and overflowing. My husband and I limped to the front of the church and the service began. We tried to make it a happy service as we were celebrating the life of my children and Ann - they are still alive. At this time my sister Karen received another vision - she could see Shannen, Niall and other children all in a circle, as we sang the songs of praise they were dancing and laughing. Ann was standing just outside the circle and she was laughing. This was confirmation to me, that my children were alive, more than ever and they were happy.

My husband and I moved into my parent's home as we just could not bear to go home. It was a difficult period and I would like to say that I was at peace and that a miracle happened - but nothing did happen. Life continued and our lives were totally shattered. If you can imagine a mirror that is broken - that is our life - it is now shattered into tiny pieces - we now have to pick up each piece, one at a time and place it back where it fell out. At times sticking the piece in the wrong place and having to take it out, deal with the trauma again and stick the piece back in the right place. I would like to say that God came down and saved the day, but he didn't. I would like to say I felt God's presence with me all the time and I had peace that surpassed all understanding - but I didn't.

It was while we were staying at my mom's house that I received a vision of Shannen. She came down to me from heaven and I just hugged her and would not let her go. I could not believe that I could feel her although she was in spirit. I felt every part of her face. I looked at her and I said "Shannen, I miss you so much," and she replied, "I know." Then I asked her, "Shannen please tell me what Jesus looks like," and she replied "Oh Mama, he has light in his hair." And with that she disappeared. I was so pleased to have seen and touched my daughter, but it was bitter-sweet.

After staying a couple of weeks in my parents' house my husband and I knew it was time to go home. To an empty house; to a house that we had left in such high spirits and now had to return just the two of us. Three little boxes with ashes; it was devastating. I cannot tell you the emotions that went through me that day. I got to the stage where I would put every television on in the house, including all the radios so that there was a constant noise. I could not have silence in the house. I could not enter my children's rooms. They had left them in a mess because we had just packed to go on holiday. Oh the heartache, I cannot even describe it. It is a physical pain that you feel in your heart - well your heart is broken.

I remember waking up in the night in a panic, wondering who was brushing my babies' hair and their teeth and watching them. The things you suddenly think of when you are sleeping. However, my mom received a beautiful vision. In her vision Jesus himself came down from heaven, he picked up my little boy in his arms, immediately, confirming he died on impact, Jesus walked over to Shannen and waited for her (as she was dying in my arms - thank God I could be with my daughter when she died) then when she died he picked her up, Jesus then walked over to Ann and also waited for her death and then they all went up to heaven. I have never told my mom in which order the children died in and where the children were when they died, however, in the vision my mom had the exact sequence of deaths and the exact place where Jesus collected them correct, thus confirming the vision is true. This was such a relief to me as a mother - you just think, *how did my children find their way to heaven?* However, Jesus personally came and collected them - what a blessing and a privilege. I would have loved to have seen my children's face when they saw Jesus, they knew him personally and they would have known exactly who he was.

A couple of months after the accident we had to go back to Durban to attend the State court case against the driver for negligent driving and also driving an unworthy vehicle. The vehicle that hit us was coming in the opposite direction of the highway - it was raining - the driver lost control of the truck and hit us on the side. My husband's door was ripped off and the whole side of our vehicle was a huge crumpled mess. The policeman who arrived at the scene of the accident was a Christian and the first words he said to my husband and I was, "You should all be dead, it is up to you to find out *why* you lived." Those words have never left me...they say the size of your problem is related to the size of your destiny - so I have decided mine is huge!

I must mention here that my dad and I were allowed to go in and sit on the court hearing. I had to look at the driver of the other vehicle and I made a decision to forgive that man. I had to release the anger and I had to forgive. By the end of the court case I had, with God's grace, managed to forgive this man. Although to be honest my anger with God was a lot worse and that has taken me years to do, to forgive God for allowing my children to die in the way they did has taken me years to forgive God. However, I do not feel guilty, God knows me and I cannot hide my heart from him, but I am trying. I always tell people I am a "work in progress." To forgive is to surrender your right to get even.

God did allow my children to go to heaven that day. I will only know when I am in heaven *why*. I will not find out on earth the why, but I know I will find out in heaven - the destiny of my children is too big for my little earthly mind to comprehend and even if God did tell me I would not understand. After six years I can only say now, "Praise the God who gives and takes away."

Grief is just a huge process that does not go away. When you lose a child you lose a part of you - therefore two parts of me died in that accident. I will never be a whole person again. I will learn to cope but I will never get over the loss - *never*. Please do not tell me that time heals, it does not. Please do not tell me that all things work together for good for those who love God - do not tell me that my children had to die so that something could work together for good. Please do not give me any of those clichéd responses - please do not try and make me feel better; you can't. Please do not tell me that God looked down and saw two angels and picked them up - that's *not* my God. My God loves me unconditionally, my

God laughs with me, my God cries with me, my God collects my tears in his hands and He sits and comforts me. My God is my Father who stood next to me at the accident and put His arm around me and cried with me - that day God's heart was also broken. All you can do is encourage me, strengthen me, cry with me, laugh with me and talk about my children.

I had had a tubal ligation after my son, Niall was born as I was positive I had had all my children; a pigeon pair, never expecting for them to die before me. My doctor tried to have my tubes re-joined but unfortunately the surgery was not successful. I therefore, had to consider IVF - thinking that I fell pregnant easy with my babies that this would be easy stuff. All it would take would be one attempt and I would be pregnant; how wrong was I?

I have to tell you it was not easy and took its toll on my emotions and caused me severe depression as well as my grieving on top of the IVF procedures. I did three IVF procedures in Harare; two in Cape Town and two in Johannesburg.

It was on the fourth attempt in Cape Town that I fell pregnant with my beautiful twins. I was so excited with my growing tummy and used to show it off as much as possible. I would stand in front of my mirror and just thank God every day for my "bump." I had already received the babies names by God : Adon - short for Adonai which means Lord and Ethan which means courage and strength. I knew that the "little" twin was Ethan and the "big" twin was Adon. They were fraternal twins. Every time we saw them on the scan I would cry – and they were so funny. Adon would always be bullying Ethan and Ethan would always be trying his best to get away from Adon. Adon would just sit on his placenta and kick his little brother. I have some fantastic photos of them inside me with their little feet, little hands and little heads – so sweet. I just fell in love with them so much and used to talk to them all the time.

I then got a flu virus and my lungs swelled up to an enormous size and were about to stop working. Here I was pregnant with twins and only hours away from death. I was slowly suffocating to death. My specialist admitted me to ICU at St. Anne's and I was put on heavy dose of steroids, had oxygen and bleeping machines all around me. The whole time the twins were of the utmost importance and were being checked all the time. The twins were never affected in any way and my oxygen levels were kept up so that the babies would receive the correct amount of oxygen. I was actually not worried about my own health; all I was worried about was my twins. The specialist did not believe I was going to make it through the night and thought I would be dead in the morning. That night I had a spiritual battle; I did not sleep at all. I read my bible all night and as soon as I stopped reading my bible an incredible black cloud would descend on me and I knew I had to keep reading to keep this blackness away from me. I finally had something to live for. I had my beautiful twins that I was going to give birth to and I had a future again. I was determined to live.

I did survive the night and my twins survived as well. In fact they grew so much whilst I was in hospital, I was delighted when I was discharged. That happened in May/June 2007.

However, that was short lived. On July 26, I went for a scan to check on the blood flow to the twins. It was a normal scan. When we looked for the babies we noticed no heartbeat. There was no heartbeat. It was like I was in a recurring nightmare that would not leave me. How could there be no heartbeat? All I could think of was, *I have to bury four children, I have to bury four children* – that's all that was going through my head. My doctor was excellent with me. He was a Christian man and he just hugged me and just showed us so much compassion.

This time the grief hit me straight away. I knew what I was going to have to go through and it was sheer hell.

I had to go to the hospital and give birth to my dead babies – their due date was December 25th and so I was five months into my pregnancy when they went to heaven. I was in labor for 24 hours, all the while knowing my babies were dead. *Dead*! How could I give birth to dead babies? I cried the whole time at the hospital.

When the babies were born the doctor showed me their bodies – oh they were beautiful; they were perfect. I counted their toes, their fingers, I looked at their little ears, their eyes, their mouths – oh they were beautiful. My beautiful little twin boys were perfect and there was no explanation for their death.

The hospital took my babies away from me and cremated them for us at the hospital. Something I did not want, but actually had no say in it due to all the legalities. I never received the ashes of my twins - something that still upsets me to this day. I would have liked to have the twin's ashes and Shannen and Niall's ashes together.

I was discharged the same day and told to watch for any bleeding. The pain was so intense, I could not run away from it, I could not get away from it. I used to lie in bed; some days I would not get out of bed, I would lie in the fetal position and just wish everyone would disappear and leave me alone. I would cry all day and all night. My eyes were all puffy; I was a mess. I did not brush my hair. Eventually my parents had to come and get me dressed and cleaned up - bathe me some days, go shopping for me and pay all my bills. They did everything for me for five months. Unfortunately my husband was unable to help as he was in a bad place mentally and he was working and trying to bring in the money for us. I was in that state for five months. I used to lie in my bed and just stare at my ceiling all day, then when I had had enough of the ceiling I would stare at the tree outside. I would count the branches on the trees or I would walk around the house not knowing where I was going or what I was doing.

Then just as suddenly that I went into it, I woke up and one day and decided it was time to get out of it. I went to the doctor and was put back onto anti-depressants; they saved my life. After that I had some choices to make :

I decided to follow my Father with all my heart, mind and soul. I decided to become a better person rather than a bitter person. I decided I had to make the most of a bad situation and see the humor in everything. I had to be thankful for what I had left. I had to praise God for every day that he gave me because that was a day I could show his love to someone else. I decided to start a psychology degree to help people in the same situation as myself - wow that was a fantastic decision, I love the course! I decided to go with my God-given gift of helping children - God has given me such a heart for children and I realize what a blessing they are. I just love, loving children!

I decided I did not want to become "hard-hearted" and that I would show compassion at all times and empathize with people who have been through a bad time. And of course God has given me such strength and courage to face each day. I can only face one day at a time. I cannot think about tomorrow, my brain cannot function that far ahead, I can only think for today and for the moment.

Always remember that when you lose a child (I am also talking about an adult child) you lose a part of yourself. Therefore, a part of you is in heaven. So you have a part of yourself missing - it's gone off this earth anyway. Dead and gone as that one song goes! So you have to heal yourself, but with healing comes scarring, so you are never a whole person again. You will never return to the old *normal,* in fact *normal* is out the window. Forget normal. Nothing in your life will ever be normal again. Accept it, sorry sounds easy but it is not.

It took me a full year after the car accident for my "shock" to wear off and actually realize, *Hey my children are not coming home*! Panic just rose in me when the knowledge of the finality of their deaths went from my head to my heart and that my life is forever changed. You look ahead at your future and know the journey ahead is not the journey you planned for. You look at the future and think, *now what*?

I remember when the death of Shannen and Niall hit me. It was exactly a year after the accident - up to then I was in complete shock; walking around doing normal things, pretending everything was okay - then wham - it hit me. I curled up into a ball on the floor and I did not know what to do with myself. I walked, I ran, I even stood on my head - no, the pain was still there! I wailed and cried. An interesting thing I have learned is that "wailing" is a form of worship to God, so I am continually praising God when I wail - that's if you are thinking of God while you are wailing, obviously! However, I have to say God was not my most favorite person at this moment in my life. I was so cross with Him, I was so bitter - and I kept on thinking, *How could You put Me through this*? I was starting to get hard-hearted and bitter. Have you ever seen a bitter and angry old person - oh dear, they are not nice to be around. That was me...for probably about two years.

So do not feel guilty if you are so angry with God. God knows you, He made you - you cannot hide that you are feeling angry with Him. Too many times Christians have said to me, "Oh no, you cannot say that out loud that you are angry with God" - well to those people I am saying I was so angry with God; that I would have loved to have personally wrestled with Him. I will not hide the fact that I was angry - I was furious! Thankfully God and I worked out that problem, but it took time. Nothing that has happened in my life was an instant fix! I have buried myself in my duvet, closed all my curtains, switched off telephones and hidden the computer. Why? Who knows, but it did make me feel better at the time!

I do not like to meet new people, but it's not that I have a social phobia. Let's think about this; what is the first question these new people are going to ask me? How many children do you have? Do you realize how hard it is for me to answer that question? I still do not know how to answer it... My answer is usually that I have four children in heaven.

I also found that people did not recognize the twins as my children. Lots of people believe that because your child did not walk on this earth and that I was only five months pregnant that they can pretend the twins never existed; well I cannot. I have pictures of those twins; I dreamt about those twins, I prayed for those twins - those twins were a part of me. Of course I am going to grieve for them just the same way I have grieved for Shannen and Niall. They were just as alive as Shannen and Niall were alive to me. The pain was just as real as the accident. I will always acknowledge the twins as my children. I had gone and bought their cots, clothes and car seats.

Another thing that people have to realize is that when you lose a child you lose your future. I have completely lost my future; it's gone. What *hope* do I have for the future apart from heaven? Please remember this when you are dealing with someone who is grieving - all the hopes and dreams they had for their children are gone. My whole future is gone. I will never be a granny, I will never see my children get married, I will never see my children graduate - the list goes on and on. I struggle to go to weddings. Why? Because none of my children will get married; that is a hard fact to accept. I will never have grandchildren. Who will look after me when I am old? Those are real questions. Will I die alone with no one around me? It's a scary thought! I just pray that God takes me before I get too old! Let's hope God is reading this too!

There were some days I would just cry and I actually would not know which child I was crying for. There was so many to choose from - Shannen, Niall, Adon and Ethan. My poor mother-in-law, I haven't even got to mourning for her yet, she has to stand in line! I remember just standing in my bedroom wailing and my husband saying to me "Why you crying?" and I would answer, "I don't know." The smallest thing can set me off and I could be anywhere - that is also why I am scared to go out because I never know when I will get a trigger.

Just the other day we got our house painted. That's good, most people would say. No, it was not good. Do you know that all the fingerprints my children left on the walls were painted over? Do you know how I cried about that?

Do you know that I am still traumatized about the house being painted and it was a month ago? It was like I was painting over all the memories and trying to forget my children. It was an awful thing. Also I had not cleared out my children's rooms yet. Yes, six years after the accident I could not do it. Let's put this in perspective - for anyone who has lost a child, you will understand - if you pack your child's belongings up from their room you feel like you are betraying them and kicking them out the house. Well that's how I felt. However, when the painters came, I had to face the bedrooms. I have cried buckets of tears God says he collects your tears and I am sure I have an Olympic-sized swimming pool filled with my tears! I found all sorts of drawings and paintings. Imagine looking at your child's shoe and know that they will never wear that shoe again - the heartache just cannot be explained into words.

Now I move to anniversaries, birthdays, Christmas and Easter - all those yucky holidays for those of us who have lost loved ones! My daughter was born on the August 18^{th,} 1996; Niall was born on March 31^{st,} 1999; the twins were born on July 26^{th,} 2007; the twins birth date was really December 25^{th,} 2007; the date of the accident was December 9^{th,} 2003; Ann's birthday was November 2nd. So let's look at that; March, April, July, August, November and December are just horrible months in my life.

Healing of my emotions does not mean that I will ever forget my children. Gently I will start to move forward, never forgetting the past but just learn to cope better. I have come a long way on my journey of grief and I am glad not to be in the first stages of grief - although I do have relapses. I do have breaks with my pain every now and again. I can laugh again - thank God for my sense of humor! I am learning to make memories now. I have the privilege of working with The Michael Project which runs a children's home in Mabelreign. I teach the children three days a week - what a joy! I am not the teacher; the children teach me each and every day about life.

I have come to a place now where I have to develop a new self-identity; this is hard. I realized that I did not even know myself. I have had to find out who I am all over again. Part of this discovery has been in listening to other people and not talking - thanks to a very special friend who has taught me this lesson, the hard way! I am a new person; I will never be that same person before the accident. I am hoping that I am a better person. Sometimes I find the meaning of life in just every-day life in my daily relationships. I can see the pain in other people's eyes now and I just yearn to help them. Always remember that laughter is the best medicine as it cleanses the soul and mends the heart. I have also found that I have a new sense of direction and purpose in life. I have looked at my goals and reassessed them and become deeply connected to those I love. That is what is most important to me is to *love* one another. That is the only thing that will pass into heaven - *love.* Hold it close to your heart and love everyone you come into contact with.

So to comfort you, the mourner, you will feel like you are crazy - that's normal! You will feel like you are not really in this world - that's normal! You will never get over your loss - that's normal! You will be in the most incredible pain - that is normal! If only I had known all that... mind you I did go crazy (not sure if that is normal, but I will get back to you on that one!), and I'm proud of it! I have faced a very *abnormal* situation and survived - well so far, who knows about tomorrow.

I get cross with God...He is big enough to take it. God has made me and knows everything about me; I cannot hide my anger from Him. So I tell Him, I shout at Him and unfortunately my arms are too short to box with Him! In the story of Job, God simply wants us to *trust* Him - I am not attempting to defend God's reputation as God is big enough to do that Himself. When God answered Job in the whirlwind he basically said, "Hey Job, you know very little about running a universe so do not tell me how to run the moral universe." We are so ignorant about the wonders of the world we live in, a world we can see and touch, who are we to sit in judgment of God's moral government of the universe? Until the day we can tell the wind where to blow or we can blow up a storm - we should actually keep our mouths firmly shut about accusing God of anything. A God who is wise enough to watch over this universe is certainly wise enough to watch over me. So where was God in all of my suffering - He was and is still in *me* - not in the things that hurt me. He helps me every day to get out of bed and to fulfill my destiny.

I believe in a loving Father and although my miracles have not come, it does not stop me from believing that one day my miracle will come - even if it is in Heaven. The traumas in my life have brought my family so much together - all my extended family - I love it. I love my family dearly and I love the time I get to spend with them - God blesses me every day that I have a member of my family around me. I thank my Father every day for my family...I am like the naughty child though and am always playing pranks on everyone - we have to keep our spirits up and keep laughing.

Now you ask, how do you help someone who is hurt? There is no magic formula, there is no miracle; nothing you can say will help a suffering person. Such a person needs love, love and more love - we do not need knowledge and wisdom, we need love. We need you to stand alongside us and voice the prayers we are unable to voice. I most often found God's love in other people showing me love.

Have you ever thought that prayer means just keeping company with God? Always remember we are *human* and God is *God* - God knows our every thought and our desire. You cannot fool God. Do not try and be strong in yourself, remember that your strength comes from God .

We all have to live in light of eternity. We should have eternity in our minds and our hearts. No human can explain Heaven to us, but we have a God who reveals it to us by revealing himself to us, for in the eternal nature of

God and his ways we see a wonderful glimpse of the nature of eternity.

~ *Janine A. Milliken* ~
(From her book, *The Gift Nobody Wants*)

How quietly he
tiptoed into our world.
Softly, only a moment
he stayed
but what an imprint
his footprints have left
upon our hearts.

Author Unknown

22

Lucas Edward Eshleman

May 17, 2001 - May 20, 2001

My Story:

My pregnancy was completely normal. I took my prenatal vitamins every day, got plenty of rest and exercise, and overall felt great. I had one ultrasound during my pregnancy. I had scheduled the appointment four weeks earlier and I crossed each day off my calendar as it got closer. I loved my baby from the moment I saw the red line slowly appear on the pregnancy test. My love grew stronger with each passing day and I couldn't wait to see him or her on the monitor. I remember lying on the table filled with anticipation and excitement, while trying to ignore my full, uncomfortable bladder.

The cold gel was squeezed onto my belly and the first image we saw was confirmation that we were having a boy. There was no question, and my husband and I were filled with happiness and delight. We knew his name was going to be Lucas. He was moving, kicking and full of life. The joy I felt was immense. The sonographer measured his head, legs, heart, etc. We were told everything looked fine and I was given one small photo profiling Lucas' face. He was precious and beautiful.

We scheduled a C-section because both of my previous pregnancies had resulted in cesarean sections, after 12 to 24 hours of labor. My due date fell on May 24th which ironically is my mother's birthday. My surgery was scheduled one week prior to my due date which fell on May 17th.

When that day finally came I was anxious and excited, but scared and nervous as well. I couldn't wait to hold Lucas in my arms, to gaze into his eyes and to whisper words of love to him.

My first spinal anesthesia injection did not work. I could feel the cold, wet cotton ball as they rubbed it on my stomach. I had been through this before and I knew that I should be able to feel the sensation of it, but not the cold, wetness of it. "It's still cold." I told my doctor over and over again, to ensure that he didn't start the incision before he should. After several minutes, and several more cotton ball tests, they decided it must have been a "bad batch." I had to sit up, hang my legs over the side of the table, and bend over my knees again to receive another spinal injection. This time the cold cotton ball did not feel cold and the surgery began.

As I said, I had been through this before and I knew it wouldn't be long now. I would see my son's gorgeous face within the next few minutes. I felt a little pull and my doctor could see the head. He told me he had a lot of hair and my exhilaration grew. I squeezed my husband's hand, and out of excitement I encouraged him to peek behind the curtain so that he could see Lucas being born. Within seconds the room fell silent. There were two doctors, two nurses, an anesthesiologist and a pediatric team. Minutes before, you could hear them talking amongst themselves and getting ready to assist; now you could have heard a pin drop. After my husband snuck a peek, he became faint and had to be escorted out of the operating room. I had no idea what was going on, but naturally I knew something wasn't right. I kept asking my doctor if everything was okay. He didn't answer me but requested additional medical personnel. I laid there helpless and scared. I couldn't move. My mind was racing and the minutes seemed like hours. What was happening?!

Finally my doctor acknowledged the question I had been repeatedly asking. "You're baby appears to have some deformities and we are trying to figure it out." I said nothing. I couldn't see, but I sensed that they were frantically in the process of cleaning Lucas. I could hear him crying; his beautiful, individual sound. Little did I know, I wouldn't hear his cry again.

As the doctors were finishing up my surgery, they brought Lucas over beside my head so that I could admire him. He was beautiful with brown hair and dark brown eyes. I tried to soothe him with my voice. I told him that I loved him as they rushed him out of the room. I was told he was turning gray and that they needed to get him to the NICU.

I lay there frightened as I was tugged and pulled at, and put back together again. The emotions I felt were overwhelming. I was dazed and confused. The hospital staff was counting supplies and tools, but the room was no longer upbeat and optimistic as it had been in the beginning. How could my emotions change so drastically, so quickly?

They took me to the recovery room, only this time I didn't have a baby waiting for me. My mom came in, her eyes full of worry and concern. I felt sad for her as this should have been a happy moment in her life. What was happening? I wanted my baby and I wanted him now! Although I was worried, I was sure he would be fine. I knew the NICU would give him what he needed and he would come home with us. I was so wrong.

I lost all track of time but once I was able to wiggle my toes, I was helped into a wheelchair and wheeled down the hall to see Lucas. The nurses took a few Polaroid photos. Looking back at those photos, I had a big smile on my face. I was ecstatic to see Lucas and to be able to hold his hand. I clearly didn't comprehend how serious Lucas' condition was. He was hooked up to several machines with tubes taped to him from head to toe. Lucas squeezed my finger and there we sat for the next hour or so. It was hard to go back to my hospital room without him. This is not how it was supposed to go.

Lucas was born at 10:56 a.m. It was now midnight and the doctors still didn't have any answers. Finally at 2 a.m. the next morning, a doctor I had never met before came in and sat down at the end of my bed. He had white hair and soft eyes. Lucas was born with Aperts Syndrome and a serious heart defect. He was in the process of being transferred to a bigger hospital about 40 miles south. I was exhausted, but couldn't sleep. My son was alone in an ambulance, experiencing sounds and sensations that were foreign to him. *Was he wondering where I was? Was he cold? Hungry? Scared? And was he missing me as much as I was missing him?* Oh how I wanted to rewind time and be back home; in my warm bed, feeling Lucas's carefree kicking and movement.

I was scheduled to stay in the hospital for three nights, but they discharged me the very next day so that I could take the 55-minute drive to see Lucas. The hospital he was at didn't have any room available for me so my husband and I stayed at a Ronald McDonald House nearby. The second day there I woke up in extreme pain. My body was ready to feed Lucas and my breasts were as hard as rocks. But there was no relief. Lucas had to be fed through tubes because he was born with a cleft palette. The roof of his mouth didn't develop normally (which left an opening in the palate that goes through to the nasal cavity). The tubes interfered with his voice box therefore we couldn't hear his voice. The heat lamps seemed to bother his sensitive skin and he was uncomfortable at times. We would see him crying but there was no sound. We could see his silent cry.

We gowned up, washed our hands and arms all the way up to our elbows and visited him as often as we could.

We met with a team of doctors and it didn't look good. They drew pictures of the heart trying to describe the defect.

Lucas died on May 20th. During his short time on Earth he showed his love in amazing ways. He was pronounced dead at 6:08 pm as I was holding him and I was crying hysterically. All of the sudden he slowly opened his eyes and looked up at me. My hysteria eased as I looked into his dark eyes. “If he's gone, why is he looking at me?” I asked the doctor who checked his pulse again and was stunned. Lucas was alive. I imagined him speaking to God, telling him that his mommy wasn't ready yet and to please give him just a little more time.

For the next two hours, my husband and I cradled him between us, and whispered our goodbyes. I told him I'd be okay and that he could go. And he did. His Spirit left his body and we undeniably felt the difference when it did. There was no question that he was no longer there in our arms. It was only his earthly shell. He was gone.

The nurse came and gently took him from us. I fell into my husband's chest and let out a wailing cry like never before. This was not how it was suppose to go! My dad drove us home that night. Because I had been discharged from the hospital three days early, my body hadn't had time to heal. And every little bump we hit on the 60-minute drive home brought pain and discomfort. My breasts were leaking and my body longed to feed my son. How could this be? I was producing precious milk for my precious baby and he couldn't benefit from it. I was in physical and emotional pain and didn't know where to put it.

When I walked into our home, my daughters Paige and Marrae (5- and 2-years-old at the time) greeted me with hugs and kisses. It was a joy to see them, and my face almost cracked when I smiled. I cried myself to sleep that night and several nights thereafter.

Ironically on May 24th, my mother's birthday, we were attending Lucas' funeral. I could see the worry and concern in my mom's eyes. I felt sad because this should have been a happy day for her.

The hardest thing for me was/is:

In the beginning I had mixed emotions when I saw pregnant women and mothers with new babies. I felt sincerely happy for them yet envious at the same time.

Another hard thing is missing him every day. Missing the smiles I will never see or the hugs I will never feel. The never-ending unanswered questions; What he would look like? What he would be doing? What milestones would he be at? Starting third grade? Chasing girls? How many tooth-fairy visits would he have had? What would his likes or dislikes be? Would he like his peas and carrots or would he hate them? Would he be playing video games with his brothers or playing school with his sisters? What would his voice sound like today?

Helpful things that family and friends did that I will forever be grateful for:

A lot of our family members where there with us during Lucas' last hours and we appreciated them being there.

The Neonatal Intensive Care Unit staff at Maine Medical Center in Portland, Maine; they were wonderful in every way. They took photos for us, and supplied cameras so that we could have pictures of Lucas to treasure. They gave us our privacy while we said goodbye and supplied us with a gift box full of his things. We have a lock of his hair, his pacifier, the clothes he was wearing and his baby footprints.

My mom took a week off to stay with me while I was healing, physically and emotionally. She was amazing and helped with everything that needed to be done on a daily basis.

My brother and some of his friends helped move all of the baby furniture and clothes out of our house before we got home. It would have been even more painful to go home and look at an empty crib or have to look at all the baby clothes that Lucas wouldn't get to wear.

My dad gave Lucas a teddy bear and wrote a nice note to him. It was sweet.

My in-laws were there for us and helped with all the funeral arrangements, which was a huge help. I was in such a daze that I hardly remember it. I don't know what we would've done without them.

A friend of ours, Angela, brought over a nice hot meal one evening. She had prepared lasagna, salad, bread and dessert. It was so thoughtful of her and we loved not having to think about what to make for dinner that evening.

My dear friend, Sylvia, answered questions from work clients who called in to see how my new baby and I were doing. She was the one who explained (so that I didn't have to) that there were complications and that Lucas had passed. I know it wasn't easy for her and I will always appreciate her courage during that time.

Things that have helped me cope and deal with the heartache:

Things that have help ease my pain are: God, praying, writing letters to Lucas, online Infant Loss support groups, reading other peoples stories, helping and supporting others during difficult times with words of comfort, books, books and more books. Also reading books on anything spiritual in nature, grief, life after death, and reading related poems. Talking about Lucas and keeping his memory alive. And keeping a journal helps me to release painful emotions.

What I have learned from this:

I feel as though I have grown and am continually trying to become the best person I can be. I am learning to live in and appreciate the present moment *now.* I appreciate my children and hearing the sound of their voices. I am thankful for every day I have with them. Because of my experience and losing Lucas, my entire way of thinking changed. With the support of my husband, I made a difficult decision and decided to end my career as a successful office manager working for a global corporation, to being a stay-at-home Mom. It's not always easy. Our entire way of living changed. We now cut coupons and buy almost everything used. It was a frightening choice, but I didn't want to miss out on one minute of my children's lives. It goes by so fast and the time can be so short. I was working nine hours a day and was missing so much! I have gained that back and feel so fortunate and blessed on a daily basis because of it.

How I keep my infant's memory alive:

I include a small photo of Lucas in the bottom corner of our family Christmas card each year. We also celebrate his birthday each year with cake and ice cream. We sing Happy Birthday to him, and blow out candles. And I have a cabinet with his things in our dining room. His framed birth certificate, stuffed animals, photos, dried flowers, his baby rattles, angel figurines; anything that reminds us of Lucas goes into this cabinet.

Additional words to help others dealing with the loss of their infant:

Take your time healing. Remember that everyone is different. If you feel like crying, cry. Feel your emotions and let them pass when you're ready. Try to remain positive and keep the faith, knowing that even though we as humans cannot possibly understand, there is a source greater than us and that with love all will one day fall into place. Helping and supporting others in need will also help with your healing. Let your story inspire and bring comfort to others.

~ Melissa Eshleman ~

"He was. He existed. He was a very small person that touched our lives in a powerful way... Losing Joe did not ultimately rip my life apart, but rather made me stronger, emotionally and spiritually."

Jan Wolfe Rosales, Author of Given In Love But Not Mine To Keep: Finding Strength In The Loss Of A Newborn Child

Afterword

You are to be commended for finishing *Always Within; Grieving the Loss of Your Infant.* Although nothing will erase your grief, you have just taken an important step towards healing. Taking it one step at a time, and day-by-day will lead you on a path of awakening and solace. Grief can sometimes persist and linger. It can return when we least expect it and catch us off guard, therefore, you should keep this book along with other helpful tools handy. Check out the resource section and find additional help if needed. Be patient with yourself and allow yourself time to heal on your own terms and timetable. There is no right or wrong way to grieve. Do what feels right for you. Have faith and be kind to yourself. I wish you peace and comfort.

About Melissa Eshleman

In 2001 Melissa had to say goodbye to her infant son Lucas, who was born with Apert's Syndrome and a heart defect.

Melissa founded Find Your Way Publishing, Inc. with the dream of helping others by publishing works to help people "find their way" in all areas of their lives. Melissa is a member of several infant loss groups and plans on donating several of these books to hospitals around the country.

Melissa and her husband are blessed to have four wonderful children in their lives that keep them very busy. Melissa is currently working on several projects and book ideas. She enjoys reading, writing, being outdoors, studying the Bible, spending time with her loved ones and learning and applying tools for spiritual growth.

Resources

These are just some of the resources I have come across over the years. There are so many helpful groups and organizations available to offer support to bereaved parents. Please keep in mind that this is just a small listing. The resources available are unlimited. Where there is help, there is hope.

Support & Resources

A.M.E.N.D. (Aiding a Mother and Father Experiencing Neonatal Death)
1559 Ville Rosa
Hazelwood, MO 63042
Phone: (314) 291-0892

A Place to Remember
1885 University Avenue, Suite 110
Saint Paul, MN 55104
Phone: (800) 631-0973
Website: www.aplacetoremember.com

American SIDS Institute
528 Raven Way
Naples, FL 34110
Phone: (239) 431-5425
Fax: (239) 431-5536
Website: www.sids.org

Bereaved Parents of the USA
National Office
Post Office Box 95
Park Forest, IL 60466
Phone: (708) 748-7866
Website: www.bereavedparentsusa.org

CJ Foundation for SIDS
HUMC: WFAN Pediatric Center
30 Prospect Avenue
Hackensack, NJ 07601
Tel: (201) 996-5301
Toll Free: (888) 8CJ-SIDS
Fax: (201) 996-5326
Email: info@cjsids.org
Web site: www.cjsids.org

Compassionate Friends
National Office
P.O. Box 3696
Oak Brook IL 60522-3696
Phone: (630) 990-0010
Fax: (630) 990-0246
Website: www.compassionatefriends.org

Faces of Loss, Faces of Hope
Putting a face on miscarriage, stillbirth, and infant loss
PO Box 26131
Minneapolis, MN 55426
Website: www.facesofloss.com

First Candle (previously SIDS Alliance)
1314 Bedford Avenue,
Suite 210
Baltimore, MD 21208
Phone: (800) 221-7437
Email: info@firstcandle.org
Website: www.firstcandle.org

Heartstrings
Pregnancy & Infant Loss Support
PO Box 10825, Greensboro, NC 27404-0825
Phone: (336) 335-9931
Email: info@heartstringssupport.org
Website: www.heartstringssupport.org

Miss Foundation
P.O. Box 5333
Peoria, Arizona 85385
Phone: (623) 979-1000
Fax: (623) 979-1001
Website: www.missfoundation.org

The National Sudden and Unexpected Infant/Child Death and Pregnancy Loss Resource Center
Georgetown University
Box 571272
Washington, DC 20057-1272
Phone: (866) 866-7437
Fax: (202) 784-9777
E-mail: info@sidscenter.org
Website: www.sidscenter.org

Pregnancy and Infant Loss Center
1421 E. Wayzata Blvd.
Wayzata, MN 55391
Phone: (612) 473-9372

Remembering Our Babies
3210 Ewing Drive
Manvel, TX 77578
Website: www.october15th.com

Rowan Tree Foundation
PO Box 393
Parker, CO 80134
Phone: (303) 378-4300
Website: www.rowantreefoundation.org

Share Pregnancy & Infant Loss Support, Inc.
The National Share Office
402 Jackson Street
St. Charles, MO 63301
Phone: (636) 947-6164 or (800) 821-6819
Fax: (636) 947-7486
Website: www.nationalshare.org

Internet Resources

http://community.babycenter.com/groups/a15155/miscarriage_stillbirth_infant_loss_support

http://www.facebook.com/pages/Pregnancy-Infant-Loss/136487461035

http://health.groups.yahoo.com/group/angelbabies4/

http://health.groups.yahoo.com/group/Infant-Loss/

www.myspace.com/allangelbabies

www.nowisleep.com

Resources for Keepsakes

A Place To Remember
1885 University Avenue
Suite 110
Saint Paul, MN USA 55104
Phone: (800) 631-0973
FAX (651)-645-4780
Website: www.aplacetoremember.com

Angel Names Association
PO Box 423
Saratoga Springs, New York 12866
Website: www.angelnames.org

La Belle Dame
2476 TransCanada Highway
Flat River, PEI
C0A 1B0
Canada
Website: www.labelledame.com

My Forever Child
P.O. Box 541
East Northport, NY 11731
Phone: (888) 325-2828
Website: www.myforeverchild.com

Metal Stamped Memories
Website: www.metalstampedmemories.com
Remembering Our Babies
3210 Ewing Drive
Manvel, TX 77578
Website: www.rememberingourbabies.net

The Comfort Company
1144 East State Street, Suite #A214
Geneva, IL 60134
Phone: (888) 265-2822
Website: www.thecomfortcompany.net

Books

An Empty Cradle, a Full Heart: Reflections for Mothers and Fathers After Miscarriage, Stillbirth, or Infant Death by Christine O'Keeffe Lafser

Empty Arms: Coping After Miscarriage, Stillbirth and Infant Death by Sherokee Ilse

Empty Cradle, Broken Heart, Revised Edition: Surviving the Death of Your Baby by Deborah L. Davis

Given In Love But Not Mine To Keep: Finding Strength In The Loss Of A Newborn Child by Jan Wolfe Rosales

Grieving the Child I Never Knew by Kathe Wunnenberg

Heaven's Child: Recovering from the loss of an infant by Christine K. Ikenberry

Hope is Like the Sun: Finding Hope and Healing After Miscarriage, Stillbirth, or Infant Death by Lisa Church

In A Heartbeat by Dawn Siegrist Waltman

Life Touches Life: A Mother's Story of Stillbirth and Healing by Lorraine Ash

Losing Malcolm: A Mother's Journey Through Grief by Carol Henderson

Pregnancy After a Loss: A Guide to Pregnancy After a Miscarriage, Stillbirth, or Infant Death by Carol Cirulli Lanham

Stolen Angels: 25 Stories of Hope After Pregnancy or Infant Loss by Sharee G. Moore

Tender Fingerprints by Brad Stetson

Waiting with Gabriel: A Story of Cherishing a Baby's Brief Life by Amy Kuebelbeck

What Was Lost: A Christian Journey Through Miscarriage by Elise Erikson Barrett

Songs

All My Tears ~ Selah

Angels Among US - Alabama

Beauty From Pain ~ Superchick

Before The Morning ~ Josh Wilson

Broken ~ Lindsey Haun

Cradle of Wings - In Memory ~ Pam Armstrong and Susan Armstrong Lunn

Fly ~ Celine Dion

Glory Baby ~ Watermark

Godspeed (Sweet Dreams) ~ Dixie Chicks

Goodbye For Now ~ Kathy Troccoli

Heaven Was Needing A Hero ~ Jo Dee Messina

Held ~ Natalie Grant

Hello, Goodbye ~ Michael W. Smith

How Come The World Won't Stop ~ Anastacia

I Believe ~ Diamond Rio

I Can Only Imagine ~ Mercy Me

I Knew I loved You ~ Savage Garden

I Will Carry You (Audrey's Song) ~ Selah

In The Arms Of an Angel ~ Sarah McLaughlin

My Heart Will Go On ~ Celine Dion

My Name ~ George Canyon

One More Day With You ~ Diamond Rio

Precious Child ~ Karen Taylor Good

Smallest, Wingless ~ Craig Cardiff

Still ~ Gerrit Hofsink

To Where You Are ~ Josh Groban

When I Look To The Sky ~ Train

Who You'd Be Today ~ Kenny Chesney

Disclaimer

The purpose of this book is to provide information about the subject matter covered. The author and publisher shall have neither liability nor responsibility to any person or entity with respect to any loss or damage caused, or alleged to have been caused, directly or indirectly, by the information contained in this book. The stories contained in this book are the contributor's recollections of their experiences. This book is not intended nor is it implied to be a substitute for professional medical advice, and any medical advice, and any medical information contained in this book is not intended to be diagnostic or treatment in any way. The author and publisher are not engaged in rendering medical, psychological or any other professional services. If medical, psychological or other expert assistance is required, please talk to your physician and locate the services of a competent professional. If you do not wish to be bound by the above, you may return this book along with a copy of the receipt to the publisher for a full refund.

Always Within

Grieving the Loss of Your Infant

Quick Order Form

Fax orders: 207-514-0438.

Telephone orders: 207-514-0575

Internet orders: www.findyourwaypublishing.com

Postal orders: Find Your Way Publishing, Inc.
PO Box 667
Norway, ME 04268
USA

Please include:

Name of book: ______________________________

Quantity: ______________________________

Name: ______________________________

Address: ______________________________

City: ______________________________

State: ______________________________

Zip: ______________________________

Telephone: ______________________________

Email address: ______________________________

Thank You!

Always Within

Grieving the Loss of Your Infant

Quick Order Form

Fax orders:	207-514-0438.
Telephone orders:	207-514-0575
Internet orders:	www.findyourwaypublishing.com
Postal orders:	Find Your Way Publishing, Inc. PO Box 667 Norway, ME 04268 USA

Please include:

Name of book: ______________________________

Quantity: ______________________________

Name: ______________________________

Address: ______________________________

City: ______________________________

State: ______________________________

Zip: ______________________________

Telephone: ______________________________

Email address: ______________________________

Thank You!

CPSIA information can be obtained
at www.ICGtesting.com
Printed in the USA
LVOW04s1937130916
504425LV00001B/66/P